SHADE GARDENING

Created and designed by the editorial staff of ORTHO BOOKS

Edited by Ken Burke

Written by A. Cort Sinnes

Designed by James Stockton

Ortho Books

Publisher
Robert L. Iacopi

Editorial Director
Min S. Yee

Managing Editor
Anne Coolman

Horticultural Editor
Michael D. Smith

Senior Editor
Kenneth R. Burke

Production Manager
Laurie S. Blackman

Horticulturists
Michael D. McKinley
Deni W. Stein

Editors
Barbara J. Ferguson
Susan M. Lammers
Sally W. Smith

Production Assistants
Darcie S. Furlan
Julia W. Hall

National Sales Manager
Garry P. Wellman

Operations/Distribution
William T. Pletcher

Operations Assistant
Donna M. White

Administrative Assistant
Georgiann Wright

Address all inquiries to:
Ortho Books
Chevron Chemical Company
Consumer Products Division
575 Market Street
San Francisco, CA 94105

First Printing in August, 1982

1 2 3 4 5 6 7 8 9

82 83 84 85 86 87

ISBN 0-89721-005-0

Library of Congress Catalog Card
Number 82-82159

Chevron Chemical Company
575 Market Street, San Francisco, CA 94105

Front cover:
Michael Landis
Beds of pink, white, red, and purple
impatiens flourish in the shade of
paperbark birch trees.

Back cover:
Michael McKinley
Flame azaleas, rhododendrons, and
calendulaceum put on a spectacular
display of May color at the Arnold
Arboretum, Jamaica Plains,
Massachusetts.

Title page:
Michael McKinley
Early May brings a riot of color to this
shady spot in a Long Island garden.
Plants include Persian lilacs,
rhododendrons, and orange Exbury
azaleas in the background.

Consultants:
Frederick McGourdy, Dennis Westler
Contributing writer and consultant:
Al Horton

Acknowledgments:
Andropogon Associates, L.A.,
Philadelphia, PA
The Arnold Arboretum, Jamaica
Plains, MA
Dr. Ernesta Ballard, Philadelphia, PA
David Benner, New Hope, PA
The Birmingham Botanic Garden,
Birmingham, AL
The Boerner Botanical Gardens of
Whitnall Park, Hales Corner, WI
F.H. Cabot, Cold Spring, NY
Robert Chesnut, L.A.,
Charleston, SC
James David, L.A., Austin, TX
Harold Epstein, Larchmont, NY
Barbara Fealy, L.A., Portland, OR
Barry Ferguson Designs,
Oyster Bay, NY
H. Lincoln Foster, Falls Village, CN
Dan Franklin, L.A., Atlanta, GA
Christopher C. Friedrichs, L.A., New
Orleans, LA
Garden in the Woods,
Framingham, MA
Katherine Hull, Manchester, MA
Carlton B. Lees, L.A.
Frederick and Mary Ann McGourty,
Norfolk, CN
Oehme, Van Sweden & Associates,
L.A., Washington, DC
Old Westbury Gardens,
Westbury, NY
Panfield Nurseries, Cold Spring
Harbor, NY
Planting Fields Arboretum, Oyster
Bay, NY
Rosedown Gardens, Bellevue, WA
Roy Davidson, Seattle, WA
Strybing Arboretum,
San Francisco, CA
Jane Wilson Photo Research,
Hillsborough, CA

Typography by Vera Allen, Castro
Valley, CA
Color separations by Color Tech,
Redwood City, CA
Copy editing and additional writing by
Jessie Wood, editcetera, Berkeley, CA

Illustrations:
Ron Hildebrand
Tinting by Cyndie Clark-Huegel

Photography:
Names of photographers in
alphabetical order are followed by
page numbers on which their work
appears. R = right, C = center, L =
left, T = top, B = bottom.
M. Baker: 33.
Josephine Coatsworth: 20C, 25T,
25C, 25BR, 71R.
Derek Fell: 15T, 15CL, 15CR, 17B,
18BR, 19T, 19C, 19BL, 20BR, 21T,
21C, 22C, 22BL, 23T, 24BL, 24BR,
25BL, 36, 37T, 58B, 59R, 62R, 63BR,
64BR, 66R, 67C, 70L, 70R, 72R,
74BR, 75L, 77R, 79L, 79R, 80L, 81R,
82L, 82C, 82R, 83L, 85R, 86R, 87L,
89R, 90L, 91L.
Pamela Harper: 15BR, 23C, 24CR,
38, 59L, 64TR, 69TR, 71L, 72C, 73L,
73R, 74TR, 76BL, 76L, 77L, 78L,
81BL, 84TL, 84BL, 85L, 85C, 86L,
91C, 92R, 94L.
Susan Lammers: 21BR, 88C, 88R.
Michael Landis: 16BL, 68BL, 75R,
89C.
Fred Lyon: 29B.
Michael McKinley: 4, 5, 6, 7, 8, 9, 12,
16TL, 16TR, 16BR, 17T, 18T, 20BL,
21BL, 23BL, 23BR, 24T, 28T, 28B,
29T, 31, 35T, 35B, 41T, 46, 50B, 51,
52T, 52B, 53L, 53R, 54T, 54R, 56T,
56B, 57T, 57B, 58T, 61, 63L, 63TR,
64L, 65L, 65R, 67L, 68TL, 68R, 69L,
69BR, 70C, 71C, 72L, 73C, 74L,
76TL, 76R, 78C, 78R, 81TL, 83R,
86C, 87R, 88L, 89L, 91R, 92L, 92C,
93L, 93R.
Jack Napton: 62L, 66L.
Kurt Reynolds: 20T, 66C, 84TL, 94R.
George Taloumis: 37B, 41B, 42, 80R.
Tom Tracy: 54C.
Wolf von dem Bussche: 50T.

SHADE GARDENING

Many
SHADES OF SUCCESS

Consider that shady spot in your garden as a challenge and an asset, learn the special needs of shade-loving plants, and your former problem spot becomes a cool, attractive, and refreshing haven to enjoy on a summer day.

The cooling effect of a shade garden in midsummer is one of life's refreshing pleasures. The combination of shades of leafy green and the dappled effect of sunlight and shadow acts as a magnet, drawing anyone within sight to stop and rest for a moment.

Shade in the yard need not be a deterrent to gardening. Simply consider shade gardening an asset, rather than a problem to overcome, and you will easily produce an attractive outdoor environment. To help gardeners solve their shade problems, we have taken an honest look at both the positive and the negative aspects of shade, and offer suggestions on ways to capitalize on the best features and to minimize the problems. Here is all the information you will need for gardening in the shade, whether in light shade with dappled sunlight under tall trees, or in an area of deep shade created by walls and overhangs. We help you identify what type of shade is present in your garden, and outline the basic needs of shade plants and how to meet those needs.

There are ways to reduce the amount of shade to allow more sunlight and air circulation into the garden. And if you want to add shade to your garden, we offer suggestions on ways to create it with shade structures, and also present a brief review of the best shade trees.

Follow our suggestions for planting with color to brighten even the shadiest area. The photographs and detailed care information in the *Plant Selection Guide* introduce you to the long and varied list of shade plants, including shrubs, trees, ground covers, and annual and perennial flowers. As you will see, gardening in the shade can be as interesting and rewarding as it is in the sun.

Left: Shade is the magic ingredient that lends this woodland scene its special charm. Above: Everyone who passes this small garden on a warm summer day feels the welcoming power of a shady place.

How shade plants are different

Plants use the energy from sunlight to produce the food they need in order to grow. In this sense, all plants need some light to survive. But don't confuse *light* with *direct sunlight*; many plants can exist on relatively small amounts of reflected light.

As light falls on the plant's leaves, the chlorophyll (green pigment) inside the leaf uses the energy contained in the light to convert water and carbon dioxide into oxygen and sugar, which, in turn, power the plant's growth process. The plant receives most of its water from beneath the surface of the soil; the carbon dioxide is taken from the air surrounding the plant and processed through the pores of the leaves. This miraculous process is known as *photosynthesis*, and to this day it is not completely understood. The accompanying illustration shows how this complex system works.

Some plants are adapted to growing in shady locations. These "shade lovers" usually have more chlorophyll than plants adapted to the sun. Their leaves are more sensitive to light and better able to make use of a small amount. But the price they pay for this sensitivity is that they are not tough enough to tolerate direct sun for long. The brightness of direct sunlight bleaches their leaves to a yellow or gray color by destroying chlorophyll.

Then these bleached leaves are not able to protect themselves from the heat of the sun. On warm days, they overheat and die, either by scorching at the edges, or by developing burned spots on the surfaces that face the sun.

Even a cursory understanding of how a plant works can greatly increase your competence as a gardener—especially when it comes to gardening in the shade.

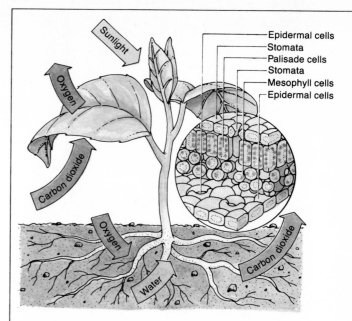

The upper and lower surfaces of a leaf are protected by epidermal cells, which are covered with a waterproof cuticle to limit the loss of water from the plant.

Water vapor, oxygen, and carbon dioxide enter and exit the leaf through apertures called stomata. The stomata are flanked by guard cells that normally open in the presence of light to permit photosynthesis and close in darkness to limit the loss of moisture.

Just beneath the upper surface is a layer of cylindrical palisade cells. This is where most of the photosynthesis takes place. In this complex process the energy of sunlight converts water and carbon dioxide into sugars. These sugars are transported throughout the plant and combined with nutrients from the soil to form the chemicals needed by the plant.

Under the palisade cells is a layer of mesophyll cells where the sugars produced by photosynthesis are stored until they are needed in other parts of the plant.

In this heavily shaded garden, plants include dwarf boxwood, Japanese aralia, and a selection of ferns.

A variety of evergreens—hollies, yews, and false cypress—perform well in the light shade cast by mature trees, giving an overall feeling of calm and tranquility. Variegated hostas ring the pool.

What plants, where

Knowing the amount of sun or shade to give a plant is a key element for the successful growth of any plant, from houseplants to fruit trees. When you narrow your selection to those plants that prefer some degree of shade, determining the amount of light required is also an important consideration. And if you expand the list further to include plants that may not actually prefer shade, but will *tolerate* it, the amount of light received becomes the most important consideration of all. Here's why:

As previously explained, some plants, because of their adaptation, need shaded conditions in order to thrive. The vast majority of plants, however, need more sunlight than shade if they are to grow in a normal, healthy manner. When a sun-loving plant is placed in a spot with the minimum acceptable level of light, it merely *maintains* itself; if it were to receive more light, it would actually grow.

When the sun-loving plant is planted in a location with less than adequate light, it will produce long, weak stems and leaves, and less foliage than normal. The plant actually stretches toward the light it needs, a phenomenon known as *etiolation*. The process of etiolation and other factors often weaken the plant to the point where it may die. A plant in this state may appear healthy for some months, but in fact it is utilizing stored carbohydrates and is slowly declining. If left in this declining state for too long, the plant may not regain its vigor even if it is transplanted to a spot with adequate light.

Shade-loving plants have an even greater response to improper light conditions. With too much sun, their leaves may wilt during the hottest part of the day, curl downward, and develop brown, burned spots. The foliage may undergo color changes, with lush greens bleaching out to unhealthy yellow colors. Left in a situation with too much light, most shade lovers will develop severely burned leaves and will eventually die.

This shaded entrance receives direct sun for only a short while in the early morning, but a fair amount of reflected light throughout the day. Clivia, a subtropical bulb, is a perfect choice for the spot, where it blooms almost continually throughout the warm months, and receives protection from winter cold.

Types of shade

One noted horticulturist recalls a college class where a professor asked the students to think of as many adjectives as they could to modify the word *shade* with regard to growing plants. When the list was compiled the students discovered that they had thought of over 200 words that could be used to describe shade: light, deep, partial, dry, dappled, and on and on.

Although a descriptive list of 200 different types of shade would be overwhelming for any practical purpose, the word *shade* should never stand alone when it is used in reference to gardening. By itself, it has only the most basic definition—the relative absence of light—and provides little help for the gardener trying to figure out the best place for a shade-loving plant.

Any description of a particular type of shade is at best an approximation open to many interpretations. The only truly scientific measurement of light, or relative lack of light, is accomplished with a light meter. And while it is possible to describe different degrees of shade using exact foot-candle measurements based on light meter readings, most gardeners and horticulturists agree that to do so would be making the problem more complex than necessary.

At the same time, there are distinct variations in shade, significant enough to make a difference in the type of plants that can be grown successfully in one set of conditions or another. To simplify the problem of describing different types of shade, we have broken it down into four categories. The plants discussed in the *Plant Selection Guide,* beginning on page 61, all carry a recommendation keyed to these classifications. Bear in mind that a garden is a place where rules can sometimes be ignored successfully, but some understanding of the types of shade commonly encountered is helpful.

Shade 1—Dappled shade
Examples: This is the type of shade produced by open trees such as birch: a moving pattern of sunlight and shade across the ground and plants. This is a fairly bright situation and the lightest shade category, but direct sun on any given area is minimal for any length of time. This is also the shade that provides the widest range of gardening possibilities, because it is hospitable to a great many shade and sun-loving plants. Lath houses also provide dappled shade.

Shade 2—Open Shade
Examples: This is the shade created by a northern exposure: a north-facing yard for as many feet out as shade is cast by an adjoining wall, fence, or building. The distance the shade is cast will vary with the season. Open shade provides good incident light, but no direct sunlight. Fiberglass-roofed patios and whitewashed greenhouses under direct sun can also be considered as providing open shade. Proximity to a south-facing wall that reflects light will greatly increase brightness in an open-shade location.

Shade 3—Medium shade
Examples: This is the shade found in north-facing locations shaded by a structure and by trees; in other words, an open-shade situation where light is further obscured by foliage and branches. A similar degree of shade also occurs under decks and stairwells and in south-facing tunnel entrances with no direct sun.

Shade 4—Dense shade
Examples: This is the deepest shade, found in north-facing tunnel entrances and north-facing sideyards. Tall walls and fences block all but the narrowest strips of incident light. There will be some reflected light. These are the most problematic areas because plant selection is severely limited. Gardening should be carefully considered in regard to how the area will be used. If it is rarely viewed, for example, something as simple as moss, stones, and gravel may be the best solution.

Types of Shade

1. Dappled shade
2. Open shade
3. Medium shade
4. Dense shade

The medium shade produced by the combination of a northern exposure and mature trees does limit the number of plants that can be grown satisfactorily—but that's no reason to have a boring garden. A combination of clipped boxwood, rhododendrons, and multicolored impatiens enlivens this area considerably.

Shade varies with your climate

If you've ever moved from one part of the country to another—particularly from north to south or vice versa—you may have been surprised at how different gardening was between the two regions. Regional differences play an important role in the location of plants in the garden. For instance, the azalea that took almost full sun in Oyster Bay, Long Island, needs plenty of protection from the elements in Louisville, Kentucky.

The reason for such differences is that the intensity of the sun increases the closer you are to the equator. Add to that basic fact the multitude of climatic influences—fog, clouds, rain, wind, and others—and you quickly realize that blanket statements concerning the type of exposure to give a plant are difficult to make.

Experience and a little common sense are your best guides in interpreting planting instructions. The instructions in this book may, for example, say to provide medium to light shade for tuberous begonias. If you live in an area that has a distinct marine influence, with frequent fog, moderate temperatures, and high humidity, you should know that the begonias could stand a great deal more sun than they could if you were living in Lubbock, Texas.

Once you get to know your own climate, and the many little climates that surround your house, the process of providing the right conditions for each plant becomes much easier.

Know your garden

For the gardener in search of plants to grow in a shaded location, some practical steps can be taken to make sure that the right plants are matched with the right conditions.

First, when you are at the nursery or garden center, confine your initial selection to those plants already growing in shaded conditions. Almost every good-sized nursery or garden center has a special place set apart for shade-loving plants. More often than not the area is a large enclosed lath house or screened-in area that simulates the growing conditions these plants prefer.

Before talking with a nursery salesperson, be sure to know as much as possible about the various microclimates and conditions in your garden. The salesperson may ask you very specific questions, such as, "Is the area under large trees?" "Are the trees deciduous or evergreen?" "Is the shade dense or dappled with sunlight?" "Does the area ever receive any sunlight during any part of the day?" By doing a little investigative work in your garden and comparing your notes with the descriptions of shade on page 8, you should be able to talk knowledgeably with nursery personnel.

The following points are important to consider.

If the planting area is under a large tree, the type of tree can make a big difference in the plants you can grow there. If the tree has a mass of surface roots, such as the sycamore, maple, or elm, or drops leaves that are

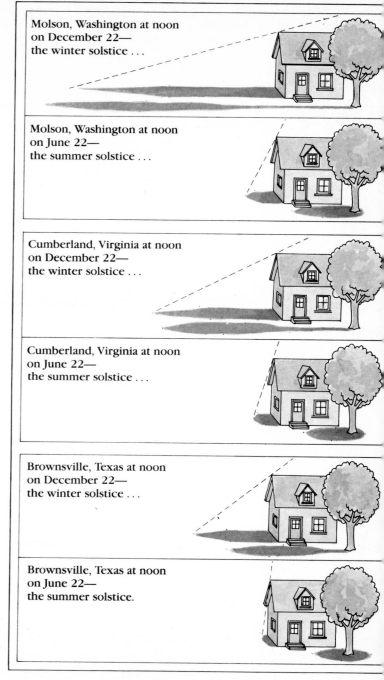

Molson, Washington at noon on December 22—the winter solstice . . .

Molson, Washington at noon on June 22—the summer solstice . . .

Cumberland, Virginia at noon on December 22—the winter solstice . . .

Cumberland, Virginia at noon on June 22—the summer solstice . . .

Brownsville, Texas at noon on December 22—the winter solstice . . .

Brownsville, Texas at noon on June 22—the summer solstice.

toxic to most plants, such as the eucalyptus, you may be advised against planting anything under the trees. Or you may want to limit the plants to containers. If the trees are deep-rooted, such as oaks and most conifers, but produce deep shade, you may be advised to do some selective thinning (see page 43) to allow more light onto the area.

If the shade in a planting area is produced by a structure, such as a house or fence, the situation is quite a bit different from that of a planting bed under mature trees. Planting beds on the north, northeast, and east sides of buildings and fences are frequently used as areas for growing shade plants. Although such areas are shaded, the amount of light they receive is usually fairly consistent, different from the play of sunlight and shadow produced by a canopy of leaves. Depending on the way

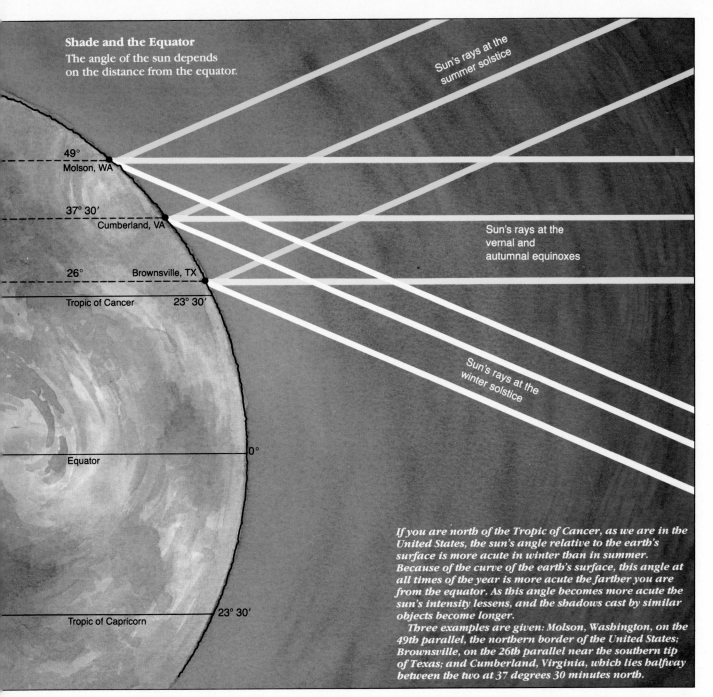

Shade and the Equator
The angle of the sun depends on the distance from the equator.

Sun's rays at the summer solstice

Sun's rays at the vernal and autumnal equinoxes

Sun's rays at the winter solstice

49°
Molson, WA

37° 30′
Cumberland, VA

26°   Brownsville, TX

Tropic of Cancer   23° 30′

0°
Equator

Tropic of Capricorn   23° 30′

If you are north of the Tropic of Cancer, as we are in the United States, the sun's angle relative to the earth's surface is more acute in winter than in summer. Because of the curve of the earth's surface, this angle at all times of the year is more acute the farther you are from the equator. As this angle becomes more acute the sun's intensity lessens, and the shadows cast by similar objects become longer.
   Three examples are given: Molson, Washington, on the 49th parallel, the northern border of the United States; Brownsville, on the 26th parallel near the southern tip of Texas; and Cumberland, Virginia, which lies halfway between the two at 37 degrees 30 minutes north.

your house is set on the lot and how far you are from the equator (see illustration), the amount of morning sun the planting area receives can vary. For shade-loving plants, there is a notable difference between the intensity of the sun at 10 o'clock in the morning and at noon, especially when light and heat are increased by a wall or fence in the background.

The old rule of thumb in such situations is that most shade-loving plants will tolerate the morning sun until noon, but after that success is variable. There are certainly many exceptions to the rule, but in general it is sound advice. Keep in mind, too, that as the sun changes its course during the year, the amount of light an area receives can change dramatically. North of the equator, the amount of sun an eastern exposure receives tends to increase as the sun approaches its peak at the sum-

mer solstice on June 22. In other words, a planting area may have the right conditions of light for shade lovers during late winter, only to have the light increase unbearably by the middle of summer.

In assessing the amount of light a particular area receives, you may discover that you can plant part of the area with true shade-loving plants and another part with plants that tolerate some shade. All plant selections for a shaded area should be made carefully with these important points in mind: Most sun-loving plants will accept some degree of shade during a portion of the day *as long as they also receive the amount of sun they need.* Shade-loving plants, on the other hand, will rapidly show signs of distress from too much direct sun (especially the hot, late afternoon sun) even though they receive adequate shade for the rest of the day.

C OLOR IN THE SHADE

Shade gardens don't have to be in muted tones of green and brown. Here are ten favorite shade-loving plants to brighten your garden with their colorful flowers or foliage.

Gardening with color is an exciting, creative endeavor, with the added satisfaction that comes from working with living, changing materials. Ideas for color schemes can be found anywhere: in a neighbor's garden, in the colors found in a single blossom, or in something as practical as the new exterior paint on your house.

The assortment of blooming shade plants is extensive, and the possible color combinations are endless. You might try using tints and shades of only one color—for example, scarlet, various tints of pink, and a deep shade of red or maroon. The various shades of "leaf" green will be a pleasant complement to the colors. Or use plants whose colors are related—red-violet, violet, and blue-violet, or yellow-orange, orange, and red-orange. Some gardeners prefer using plants whose colors complement each other—orange and blue, yellow and violet, red and green. Although these combinations are very bold, they may be ideal in a deeply shaded garden. Another color scheme is to plant a random sampling of any and every color available. This light-hearted approach to gardening with color may be termed amateurish by some, but it can be most attractive.

Flowering plants can be used to change the atmosphere of the garden. If you long for summer warmth in your cool, shady yard, try using plants with warm colors ranging from yellow to red. The colors will brighten the area and make it feel warmer. Masses of warm-colored flowers make a space appear smaller than it actually is. Shaded areas planted with colors ranging from green to violet will give the impression of coolness highlighted with subtle colors. Cool-colored plants are good for close viewing and help make an area appear larger.

Use blooming plants to highlight areas that would otherwise be unnoticeable or unappealing. Give visitors a cheery welcome with colorful plants along walkways and by doorways. If you enjoy relaxing and entertaining on your patio, decorate with pots of plants, and landscape the surrounding garden areas that can be viewed from the patio. Don't let that area under tall shade trees go to waste just because grass won't grow there. That area might be fairly sunny in the early spring before the trees leaf out. Plant some bulbs there for early color before the shade develops. Select later-blooming shade plants for color after the tree is in leaf.

When selecting your flowering plants, note which are early-, mid-, and late-season bloomers so you can plan and plant your garden for a sequence of bloom. For the greatest impact, mass or group the plants together, rather than planting them individually or in straight rows. Plan to get the most from your garden by selecting some plants that are also good cut flowers, as well as those that are fragrant. Remember to select for fragrance both indoors and out.

The following pages present ten favorite plants for color in the shade garden. Most have been chosen for their cheery flowers, but we haven't forgotten those plants with attractive foliage. Browse through these pages, enjoy the rainbow of colors available, and begin planning your shade garden. For additional blooming shade plants, see the lists on pages 55 to 59.

Small hedges of vibrant red 'Hino-Crimson' azaleas lining a stone walkway put on a splendid spring show every year, their flamboyant color contrasting vividly with the elegance of the stately home in the background. In their seemingly endless variety, rhododendrons and azaleas are among the most popular flowering shade plants.

RHODODENDRONS & AZALEAS

Probably no other group of plants elicits as much devotional praise and obsessional frustration as the genus *Rhododendron*. Where they can be grown, few plants can match their bewildering variety of striking, profuse, often brilliant flowers, outstanding form, and attractive foliage.

Rhododendron is an extensive genus, with more than 900 species and 10,000 varieties. *Azalea* is a series within the *Rhododendron* genus. There are evergreen and deciduous, small- and large-leafed, and dwarf and tall forms of these plants. The range of colors is endless, including solid and bicolored blossoms; some have a heady perfume. Depending on the variety and location, rhododendrons and azaleas bloom from late winter to midsummer.

Botanists are still arguing over exactly what anatomical characteristics separate *Azalea* from *Rhododendron*. While many azaleas are deciduous, and most rhododendrons are evergreen, both azaleas and rhododendrons have deciduous and evergreen species. A common misconception is that azaleas are always smaller in form and leaf than rhododendrons, while in fact several rhododendrons are tiny, rock-garden dwarfs with leaves smaller than any azalea. Sizes of both plants vary from 8 to 80 inches.

There is, however, one significant difference between rhododendrons and azaleas—namely, where the buds are located. Rhododendron buds are always found just above the leaf rosette; on azaleas, the buds are concealed under the bark along the entire branch. This difference influences the kind of pruning each type needs (see page 17).

The reputation of rhododendrons and azaleas as finicky, frustrating plants is misleading. If planted in a favorable location and given proper growing conditions, these plants are easy, care-free, and long-lived. The trick is in creating those favorable growing conditions.

Climate and Location

Because these plants grow best in a cool climate with high atmospheric moisture and moist, acid soil, they are difficult to grow in the central United States and in the dry desert areas of the West and Southwest. They are most widely adapted to the mid-Atlantic, northeastern, and Pacific northwestern states. Depending on species, rhododendrons and azaleas are hardy in Zones 2 to 8.

Rhododendrons and azaleas grow best in the filtered shade of high tree branches in both summer and winter. The eastern side of a sheltering structure is also a good planting location. Protection from winter sun and wind and excessive summer heat is especially important for the evergreen varieties. Due

Left: A mass of pale pink rhododendron blossoms makes a spectacular middle-distance display. This page: Azalea species shown above, center left, and bottom right. Rhododendron species shown bottom left, center right. The plants pictured on these pages are only a small sample of the hundreds of species and literally thousands of varieties of rhododendrons and azaleas. Ranging in size from 8 inches to over 6 feet, with flowers in almost every color of the rainbow and a great variety of leaf size and shape, these exotic beauties are popular wherever they can be grown. Native to the cool-climate regions of China, they are best adapted to the cooler areas of the United States, particularly the mid-Atlantic and Pacific northwestern states. Along with a mild climate, rhododendrons and azaleas prefer a moist atmosphere and moist but well-drained soil. They are especially well adapted to the protection of filtered shade beneath high tree branches.

to their shallow root systems, rhododendrons cannot reach below the frost line and transmit water to their leaves when the soil is frozen. Yet their evergreen leaves constantly transpire water, even in the coldest winter. Sun and wind at this vulnerable time can be deadly. Destructive rapid freezing and thawing can be lessened by protection from the sun during the winter. A 3-inch organic mulch applied in the fall will moderate winter soil temperatures and add needed organic matter to the soil.

Soil Requirements

Rhododendrons and azaleas require an acid soil (pH 4.5 to 6.5) that is well drained and retains moisture well. If you are amending your soil to provide these conditions, use a mixture of one-quarter soil, half organic matter (peat, composted oak leaves, ground cedar, or composted pine chips are excellent for their acid reaction), and one-quarter coarse sand. Volcanic sand, if available, is highly recommended, because it is porous and retains moisture well. Do not use sand from near the sea; it may be high in deadly salts. Adding some slow-release fertilizer is also beneficial. For serious heavy-soil problems, raised beds may be the best answer. Simply mounding the soil and planting high can improve drainage enough to mean the difference between death and survival for your rhododendrons.

If you have neutral or alkaline soil, you may want to choose another plant besides a rhododendron. Although you can acidify soil, it is a tricky operation, and you have to keep it perpetually acidic. Rhododendrons let you know when the soil has reverted to its alkaline state by declining in vigor and developing chlorosis (leaves turn yellow while the veins remain green)—actually an iron deficiency caused either by alkalinity, which makes the iron in the soil unusable, or by an actual lack of iron. The best way to acidify soil is with ferrous sulfate. A soil test report can tell you exactly how much to apply.

Moisture Requirements

Adequate atmospheric and soil moisture are essential for these plants. They will not tolerate drought for any length of time. Water rhododendrons and azaleas regularly during dry periods, but do not let the soil become soggy. Beware of water that is alkaline or high in salts. Rain water is ideal, so you might try capturing rain water to help the plants through dry periods.

A mulch helps to retain moisture and keep the roots cool. The best material is organic matter that breaks down with an acid reaction, such as oak leaves, pine needles and bark, or cedar chips. Avoid using peat as a mulch, since it forms a crust and repels water when dry; also avoid maple and elm leaves because of their heavy matting properties and alkaline reactions. Mulch to a settled depth of 2 to 3 inches, no deeper. Where flower spot or petal blight is a problem, the mulch must be replaced each year.

Rhododendrons and azaleas aren't necessarily difficult to grow, although they do have specific climate, location, soil, water, and nutrition requirements. However, they will repay the gardener's extra care with handsome, long-lasting yellow, pink, red, or salmon-colored blossoms like those shown here. All illustrations on this page are of rhododendrons.

Maintenance

Overfeeding is a common mistake. Rhododendrons and azaleas are highly sensitive to excessive levels of nitrogen around their fibrous roots. They do benefit, however, from infrequent light feeding with a fertilizer formulated for acid plants. In good garden soils, little fertilizer should be necessary. If you are using organic mulches such as wood chips, sawdust, or shredded oak leaves, additional nitrogen will be needed. Avoid manure; it is usually high in salts, to which rhododendrons are extremely sensitive.

Rhododendrons and azaleas have shallow roots, so never cultivate around them. Instead, use a mulch or gentle pulling for weed control. Encourage adequate hardening off of any new growth before the onset of winter by ceasing to apply fertilizer two months before the first frost. Send your plants into winter with plenty of moisture by giving them a good, deep watering just before the first hard freeze.

Pruning

Rhododendrons and azaleas require more grooming than pruning. The spent flower heads of rhododendrons should be removed—this is called deadheading. Tips of azaleas should be pinched off to make the plants bushier. Be careful not to take next year's buds with the flowers, though.

Your finger tips will do nicely for most of the pruning of these plants. Only older plants that have become leggy, sparse, or damaged will require a few cuts with hand pruners or loppers.

The difference between a rhododendron and an azalea lies in where the buds are located, and this causes them to need different types of pruning. Since a rhododendron bud is always found just above the leaf rosette, you must cut there, just above the bud. On an azalea, however, the buds are concealed under the bark along the entire branch. This means that you can cut anywhere along the branch and still be near a bud, which will then begin to grow.

Rhododendrons. Spent flowers must be removed from rhododendrons. If seed pods are left on the plant, they consume much of the energy that could go into flowers or leaves. Hold the branch with the faded flower in one hand, and with the other hand carefully snap off the flower head with a slight sideways pressure, taking care not to harm the growth buds below. These buds are next year's flowers and leaves. If you injure the buds, there will be no flowers next year.

If your plant is too tall to hand-pick thoroughly, little harm will be done. Try using a hose to wash the dead petals away.

Many rhododendrons tend to bloom in alternate years if they are not deadheaded.

Azaleas. Azaleas require even less pruning than rhododendrons. They should be tip-pinched, particularly when young, to produce bushier plants. Do this within a couple of weeks after the plant blooms.

What's the difference between rhododendrons and azaleas? The main significant difference between the two is that rhododendron buds are found just above the leaf rosette, while azalea buds are concealed under the bark along the entire branch. This difference is important to the gardener because it influences the type of pruning each plant needs. Aside from pruning, the cultural requirements of the two are identical. All illustrations on this page are of azaleas.

CALADIUMS

Although this South American tuber does produce small pink flowers, it is grown not for its blooms but for its striking leaves. The arrow or heart-shaped leaves are veined, edged, or mottled in numerous variations of pink, red, green, silver, and white. The plants grow about 12 inches tall and enhance any shrub border or flower bed. They also make good container plants for adding color on porches and patios.

Caladium × *hortulanum,* fancy-leaved caladiums, grow best in hot humid areas, and are hardy outdoors only in Zone 10. In other zones they are grown as annuals that are dug up just before the fall frost and stored for the winter. About two months before the air temperature will remain above 70°F, plant the tubers 1 to 2 inches deep in moist vermiculite or peat moss. When small leaves appear, transplant the young plants to 4 to 7-inch diameter containers, and move them outdoors when the weather is reliably warm (above 70°F).

Caladiums grow equally well in light or dense shade, and prefer a well-drained soil that is kept evenly moist. To maintain attractive plants and to encourage new, colorful leaves, cut off any dead leaves at the base of the leaf stalk.

Dozens of varieties of caladiums, with seemingly endless variations of color, pattern, and leaf shape, can create a colorful display that will rival any flowering plant.

CAMELLIAS

Beloved by southern and western gardeners for its large beautiful flowers in winter and spring, the common camellia, *Camellia japonica,* is a broad-leafed evergreen shrub. Its attractive, dense, shiny, dark green foliage sets off the blossoms beautifully. Camellias are very effective standing alone or planted in groups. They blend nicely with other broad-leafed evergreens, and are frequently mixed in shrub borders. Camellias commonly grow 6 to 12 feet tall, but may reach 20 feet in old age. They are sometimes single trunked and branching well up from the ground; the effect is usually a roundish, densely-foliaged mass that is nearly as broad as it is tall. From October to May, depending on the cultivar, the plants are a mass of color, ranging from white through every shade of pink to red. Individual blossoms measure from 2½ to 5 inches in diameter and may be single, semidouble, or double. They are especially attractive cut and floated in a shallow dish.

Camellias are native to China and Japan, and are hardy in Zones 8 to 10. They are available as containerized plants in your local nursery. They transplant easily into any type of soil that is high in organic matter and slightly acidic. Water when the soil is dry 3 to 4 inches deep. These plants are shallow-rooted, so don't cultivate around the roots.

C. sasanqua, the Sasanqua Camellia, is hardy to Zone 8, and blooms earlier, from autumn to early winter, than does the common camellia. This camellia is very versatile, with flowers ranging from white to pink to scarlet. It is available as a low-growing, sprawling shrub that is useful as a ground cover and espalier, and also as an upright shrub ideal for hedges or screens.

A single camellia can make a striking focal point in an oriental garden, or a group planting can produce a dramatic mass of pink to scarlet flowers.

IMPATIENS

Impatiens wallerana (Impatiens), also known as Busy Lizzie, is one of the most versatile flowering plants for shade. Use it for color under shrubs, along walkways, and tucked into corners by entranceways. Impatiens also grows readily in containers and window boxes, and provides color in hanging baskets under eaves.

Impatiens is grown as an annual, and enjoys dense to light shade. The plants bloom continually from transplanting to the first fall frost, with showy single or double flowers in shades of pink, magenta, mauve, salmon, orange, and white. Bicolored flowers are also popular. The glossy, dark green leaves frequently have a bronze hue. The erect succulent stems, 6 to 18 inches tall, are very sensitive, and wilt easily as the soil dries. Water impatiens regularly, especially in hot weather, to keep the soil moist. Fertilize lightly each month with a complete fertilizer.

Impatiens grows easily from seed when started indoors 10 to 12 weeks before planting outdoors. It also transplants well from nursery packs. For bushier plants, cut them back by a third when planting. Set the plants 10 to 15 inches apart. Impatiens grows best in well-drained, sandy soil that is high in organic matter.

A new type of impatiens, New Guinea impatiens, is available with bicolored foliage and flowers. It does best in light shade but tolerates full sun.

Impatiens, also called Busy Lizzie because it blooms so prolifically, has been a favorite of shade gardeners since the days of Queen Victoria. Its showy, colorful flowers and long blooming season contribute to its steady popularity. Low-growing varieties of this versatile plant can be used as a ground cover or in containers, and shrublike varieties can be used as a border.

HOSTAS

The lush, subtly-colored foliage of hostas makes them a welcome addition to any shade garden. Hostas, also known as plantain lilies, are ideally suited to dense to light shade around trees and shrubs and along walkways. They are late bloomers, with flower stalks of lilylike white to lilac blooms that appear from July to October. The slender to heart-shaped leaves grow in a basal rosette, and, depending on the species, the clumps may attain a height of 2½ feet and sometimes measure up to 40 inches across. The leaves may be bright or dark green, have a powdery blue cast, or be silvery white. Plants with white or yellow variegated leaves are very popular.

These perennials are hardy outdoors to Zone 3. They prefer rich, well-drained soil that is kept evenly moist. Crown rot can be a problem in soggy soils. Establish new plantings in the spring with nursery plants or young divisions. Set plants 2 to 3 feet apart. When growing hostas from seed, expect to wait at least three years for sizeable plants to develop. Hostas almost never require division, and may last 30 years or more in one spot. To propagate, divide only young plants up to three years of age, as older plants develop a tough crown that is hard to separate, and even more difficult to establish.

Snails and slugs love to feast on hostas; protect the plants with baits available at your nursery.

The most popular hostas include *H. sieboldiana,* Blue-Leaf Plantain Lily; *H. decorata,* Blunt-Leaf Plantain Lily; *H. fortunei,* Tall-Cluster Plantain Lily; *H. undulata,* Wavy-Leaf Plantain Lily; and *H. ventricosa,* Blue Plantain Lily.

For a bold, tropical feeling in a shady spot, the lush foliage and delicate white, blue, or lavender lilylike flowers of hostas are hard to beat. Native to the Orient, and particularly to Japan, hostas are long-lived and hardy, and prefer rich, moist, well-drained soil. Use them as a tall ground cover or as a hedgelike edging plant.

FUCHSIA

The colorful magenta, white, and pink blossoms of fuchsias brighten any shaded spot. Even where it can be grown only as a summer annual or a house or greenhouse plant, the common fuchsia is popular. Upright varieties reach various heights, to 10 feet, and lend themselves to use as specimens, components of shrub borders, or espaliers. Others, diminutive and trailing, are best grown in hanging planters or in raised beds. Some are pruned to a single vertical stem to form graceful standards.

The flowers appear profusely from spring to winter in the mildest areas. They are pendulous on thin stems, usually 2 to 6 inches long, and often bicolored.

The upper, waxy, backward-flaring part of the blossom (the sepals) is white or some shade of red or pink. The petals (forming the corolla) may match the sepals or be white or almost any conceivable shade of violet, purple, blue-violet, rose, pink, orange, or red. The pistil and sometimes the stamens often extend well beyond the corolla. Some corollas are tight and simple, others extravagantly ruffled and elaborate. Whatever the flowers' forms and colors, hummingbirds love them.

The leaves are thin, smooth, finely toothed, and oval or oblong, dark green above, with light green undersides. They measure from 1 to 6 inches long and at least an inch wide.

Fuchsias are native to western South America and prefer dense to light shade. Most are hardy only in Zones 9 and 10. Plant fuchsias in the spring in well-drained soil that is high in organic matter. They are very sensitive to drought, so water regularly to keep the soil moist. Fuchsias are heavy feeders; fertilize with a complete fertilizer every two weeks.

To encourage continuous blossoms, remove fading blooms, and pinch the stem tips to prevent plants from becoming leggy. Each spring, prune fuchsias back to the edge of their container, or two-thirds of the way back to the ground. Fuchsias grow fast and bloom only on new wood.

Many fuchsia species are cultivated, but the following two are particularly valuable in the shade garden.

F. magellanica (Magellan Fuchsia), native to Chile and Argentina, is used as a specimen, or as a hedge in the more temperate parts of Britain and North America. A vigorous grower, it can reach 20 feet trained on walls, but is seen more often as a shrub of 3 to 8 feet. In northern areas it is treated as a perennial. Flowers are small (1½ inch) but very profuse. Sepals are bright red and the corolla is blue. It blooms best in light to medium shade but will hold its own, in looser fashion, in deep shade. This is one of the hardiest fuchsias (to Zone 6), and one of the least finicky.

F. procumbens, from the North Island of New Zealand, is a prostrate ground cover whose many-branched, aggressively spreading stems root freely. Its small blossoms are yellow, brownish red, and green, with blue pollen. The pink fruits, ¾-inch long, are showy. It prefers moist rich soil in medium shade, and is hardy only in Zone 10.

A cascade of fuchsias in a hanging basket or a climbing fuchsia heavy with multicolored flowers enlivens any corner of the deck, patio, or garden.

COLEUS

Coleus *(Coleus × hybridus)* offer an incredible diversity of foliage colors, shapes, and sizes. The leaves may be velvety or rough and crinkled, deeply notched or round and full. They may be one solid color or several colors in varying shades of pink, red, bronze, yellow, maroon, green, and chartreuse. The square stems grow 6 to 36 inches tall. Small blue or lilac flower spikes appear throughout the summer and should be removed to conserve the plant's energy. Keep the plants bushy by periodically cutting the stems back several inches. Coleus are ideal as edging plants, as well as in flower beds, pots, and window boxes. They grow best in medium to light shade, with a rich, well-drained soil that is kept evenly moist.

Coleus propagate easily from stem cuttings. Cuttings made in the fall can be grown indoors over the winter, and planted outdoors in the spring after the late frost. They can also be grown from seeds, but no two plants will be alike. Start the seeds indoors 6 to 8 weeks before planting the seedlings outdoors. Pinch off flowers to keep flower growing vigorously. Some new cultivars stay dense without pinching back. Native to Java and the Philippines, coleus are grown as annuals in most areas of the country, since they are damaged by even the lightest frost.

In beds or hanging baskets, by itself or planted with ferns, impatiens, or begonias, the almost bewildering array of color, texture, and leaf shape ensures coleus a prominent place in the shade garden.

PRIMULAS

The genus *Primula* offers the shade gardener plants with an assortment of colors including white, magenta, pink, yellow, and orange. Some flowers are bicolored and others are fragrant. There are several hundred species, varying in height from a few inches to 3 feet tall. Flowers appear in February in mild winter areas and in April and May in northern climates. These perennials are hardy to Zone 5. The crinkly, tongue-shaped leaves form basal rosettes and are evergreen when temperatures do not drop below 15°F. For an array of spring color, plant primulas with bulbs.

New plantings can be established from nursery bedding plants, divisions, or from seeds started indoors in late winter or early spring. Primulas grow best in medium to light shade with rich, well-drained soil. Keep the soil evenly moist, and fertilize occasionally with a complete fertilizer. Divide crowded plantings every two to three years after flowering. New plants appear in the garden from self-sown seed and from surface roots, but primulas cannot be considered invasive.

The easiest-to-grow primulas are *Primula vulgaris,* English Primrose; *P. × polyanthus,* Polyanthus Primula; *P. japonica,* Japanese Primula; and *P. sieboldii.*

Massed in a large bed or edging a wooded path, the cheerful flowers of the primulas offer the shade gardener a rainbow of color.

TUBEROUS BEGONIAS

Few bulbous flowering plants are as spectacular as *Begonia tuberhybrida* (tuberous begonia). And fortunately for shade gardeners, they grow best in light shade. Vibrant single or double flowers appear all summer until frost in a variety of colors ranging from vivid red, fluorescent orange, and bright yellow to pastel apricot, pink, and pure white. They enhance and brighten any shade garden, whether in a shrub border, flower bed, windowbox, or potted on the patio. Tuberous begonias are available in numerous forms: upright plants that grow 12 to 18 inches tall; multiflora bushy varieties with small flowers; and the pendula, or hanging basket, varieties with stems trailing to 18 inches. Try the pendulas in moss-lined hanging baskets for a cool, shady spot.

Tuberous begonias are not hardy outdoors, and should be dug up each fall and replanted in the spring. Plant the tubers outdoors after the last spring frost in well-drained soil that is kept evenly moist. Fertilize with a complete fertilizer twice a month. To encourage continuous blooms, remove fading blossoms, and pinch back the stem tips if the plants become leggy.

Bring some color indoors and enjoy tuberous begonias as cut flowers. Cut the blossoms when they are fully open and float them in a shallow dish. Gently sprinkle the petals with water to make them last longer. The stems are very brittle, so handle them carefully.

Among the most versatile and colorful flowering plants in the shade garden, begonias call to mind the lavishness of Victorian estate gardening.

SHADE GARDENING PRACTICES

Less light is only the most obvious special condition of a shaded area. Picking the right plant for your particular conditions is one of the keys to heading off problems and establishing a healthy, flourishing garden in the shade.

Gardening in the shade is different from gardening in the sun. Although the good garden practices of adequate soil preparation, good watering habits, proper fertilizing, and keeping the garden clean apply to all kinds of gardening, the emphasis on some of these areas changes in the shade.

This chapter covers the basics, and explains how some of the habits you may have grown accustomed to in the sun must be modified for shade gardening. Additionally, shade gardeners must pay special attention to one other factor, namely matching the right plant with the right location. This is important in any type of gardening, but particularly important when growing plants in the shade. This matching-up process requires that you know the various conditions in your yard, as well as the requirements of the plants. In the following pages we'll give you the information you need to assess the "microclimates" in your garden; in the *Plant Selection Guide,* the requirements of each plant are noted. When you combine this information, you will be well on your way to a successful shade garden.

The importance of soil preparation

You may already know that any garden soil, from the heaviest clay to the most porous sand, benefits from regular additions of organic matter—compost, well-rotted manure, peat moss, chopped leaves, grass clippings, or any of the other widely available materials. When gardening in the shade, the extra time taken to prepare the soil will pay off handsomely in healthier plants. For all but the very best garden loam soils, you should add plenty of organic matter before planting anything, from a single azalea to a whole bed of lily-of-the-valley. If your soil is a rich loam, the addition of organic matter will improve its quality even more.

To enrich the soil and improve its aeration and drainage, spread a 2 to 4-inch layer of organic matter on the soil surface. Incorporate the material into the soil to a depth of 6 inches. If the soil is particularly heavy or you are planting a large shrub, work the soil several inches deeper. Plants with roots growing in deep rich soil will have better overall growth than those plants that are forced to compete fiercely for water and nutrients in shallow, lean soil.

Organic Matter and Soil Structure

The incorporation of quantities of organic matter into the soil results in the superior growth of plants for several reasons, the most important of which is the effect organic matter has on soil structure. The word *structure,* as it applies to soil, refers to the way the particles of soil stick together. Soil with good structure has the right amount of air space to promote both good drainage and adequate water retention. And good drainage is particularly important in shaded garden locations. Because of the absence of direct, intense sunlight, shaded soil tends to stay damp much longer than it would in a sunny location. Without excellent drainage, the gardener is likely to experience water-related growing problems such as stunted, weak plants and the presence of fungus diseases.

Creating additional shade can increase the usefulness and livability of outdoor spaces. When the owners of this house added the deck and overhead shade structure they not only improved the area for human comfort but also created a new gardening environment where the special needs of shade plants could easily be met.

Many organic materials can be used as mulch.

Organic Matter as a Mulch

Many of the organic materials used as soil amendments can also be used as mulches. The difference is in the way they are applied to the soil. A mulch is intended to lie on top of the soil, whereas a soil amendment is incorporated into the soil.

Mulches help keep the soil cool, reduce water evaporation, deter weeds, and aid in the long-term improvement of the soil. A layer of material 2 to 3 inches deep is usually recommended, and should be applied in the spring before weed growth begins and before the summer heat. For winter protection in cold winter areas, replenish the mulch before the ground freezes.

Watering

The most important rule to remember about watering is, water thoroughly, and let the soil dry out slightly between waterings. Deep soakings help plants develop deep, strong root systems, able to withstand some neglect. Frequent light waterings result in a shallow root system, and encourage disease and weed growth. Keep in mind, though, that it is easier to overwater a shade garden than it is a garden in the sun. The lack of direct sunlight reduces the amount of evaporation, resulting in the need for less frequent waterings.

If too much water stays in the root zone for too long, root growth stops, and the roots die from lack of air. The longer air is cut off, the greater the damage to the roots. Damaged roots have little defense against the entrance of rot-causing organisms, and so the plant can die of root rot.

Monitor the watering of a shade garden by inspecting the soil after a typical irrigation. Using a shovel, check to see that the water has penetrated to a depth of 4 or 5 inches. The soil should be allowed to dry out somewhat before watering again.

Be especially careful to adjust automatic sprinklers if your shade garden adjoins a lawn area. Three or four waterings a week for the lawn may be fine, but if the sprinklers also water the shade garden it's probably receiving too much moisture.

If you follow the advice concerning the addition of plenty of organic matter to the soil, you'll also avoid most problems associated with water. Soil with a good structure is hard to overwater. Because of the porosity of such soil, water, even in large amounts, will drain through, leaving the all-important air in the soil.

Although the majority of shade gardens are prone to overwatering, there are a couple of instances where the opposite is true. One is where a canopy of leaves seriously retards rain from reaching the soil. Another is where shallow-rooted trees (willows or pines) compete for water. A more common situation occurs when rain is kept from reaching a planting bed next to the house because of wide eaves or overhangs. In both cases, pay particular attention to the amount of water the plants receive throughout the year. Plants in these situations can suffer from drought conditions any time of the year.

How can you tell if your soil has good structure? The following characteristics are good indications:

■ The soil doesn't compact down after a watering or rain, and doesn't leave a hard crust on the surface as it dries.

■ The soil is easy to work using a hand spade or cultivating fork.

■ The soil is friable—it has a loose, almost "fluffy" texture.

Plants vary greatly in their requirements for air in the soil. But in looking at the air requirements of some favorite shade plants, it becomes obvious that the addition of organic matter is doubly important in shade gardening. The aeration requirement of plants is measured by the percentage of air space left in the soil after excess water from irrigation has drained away. Azaleas and most ferns have a requirement of 20 percent or more, which is considered very high. To get this level of aeration, many commercial growers grow azaleas in unmixed, coarse peat moss. Rhododendrons, begonias, and many foliage plants have air requirements of 10 to 20 percent, which is still high. Even plants classified as tolerant of low levels of aeration, such as ivy, will grow better with high percentages of air in the soil.

To reduce disease, proper spacing is essential.

Spacing in the shade

Gardeners often fudge a little (or a lot) by placing plants closer together than is recommended. Although you can sometimes get away with close planting in the sun, you definitely take your chances by doing so in the shade.

The combination of soil that stays damp for comparatively long periods of time and the reduced air circulation typical under canopies of large trees increases the possibility of disease. For this reason it is always best to err on the side of placing shade plants too far apart. The extra space allows for good air circulation (a deterrent to disease) and gives each plant the opportunity to receive its fair share of light and nutrients.

Fertilizer practices

Even though the metabolism of plants growing in the shade is slower than that of those growing in the sun, they still need a steady supply of nutrients. Monthly application of a comparatively mild complete fertilizer is a good practice when the plants are actively growing. A mild fertilizer might be a liquid fish emulsion with a 5-1-1 formulation, or a dry 5-10-5 fertilizer. (The numbers refer to the percentages of nitrogen, phosphorus, and potassium contained in the fertilizer, and are always listed in that order.)

Acid-loving plants can be given special fertilizers that have an acid reaction in the soil. These fertilizers are usually labeled "azalea and camellia food," "rhododendron and azalea food," or something similar.

No matter which fertilizer you use, always follow the directions on the label carefully. The rates and times for application have been the subject of much research and should not be taken lightly. Too much of any fertilizer can quickly damage plants.

Garden cleanup

Soil that is covered with decaying leaf litter and other garden debris is an open invitation for fungus diseases to get started. In the shaded garden, this situation spells double trouble. The cool, damp conditions are the perfect environment for the growth of many common fungus diseases. The gardener can avoid problems such as mildew, petal blight on camellias, and botrytis on azaleas by maintaining an even mulch layer and removing all other garden debris. If you still have problems, it might help to remove the mulch each year and replace it with fresh material.

Damp, cool locations are also the preferred home of snails and slugs. To keep these pests under control, minimize the places they hide and use high-quality snail and slug bait whenever an outbreak occurs.

If despite your best efforts you repeatedly have problems with fungus diseases, use one of the commercial fungicides available at your nursery. Be aware though that for the best control of some fungus diseases such as scab, the remedy should be applied *before* there is a problem. On the other hand, other fungus diseases such as mildew can be controlled with repetitive treatments either before or after they become evident. Consult your local nursery or extension agent for information about the appropriate fungicide and time to apply it. Always read and follow the label directions for each specific use.

Gardens in the shade need to be kept extra clean. Debris should be raked up and removed regularly.

CREATING AND MODIFYING SHADE

Shade-giving garden structures—from a simple canvas awning to a delicate gazebo to a leafy arbor—can give welcome, refreshing protection to tender, shade-loving plants and people alike.

The perfect conditions for outdoor living and growing are rare, even in the best of climates. The sun may be too hot at midday, the evenings may be too chilly, or strong winds may make your favorite sitting area uncomfortable. In those situations, some degree of protection is necessary if you want to get maximum use and enjoyment from your outdoor space. On the other hand, shade that covers too much of the garden, or very dense shade produced by a few overgrown trees, will need to be modified by pruning or other means for you to get full use from your garden.

This chapter will tell you what you need to know about creating protected, shady spots in your garden, and about opening up areas that are too dark.

Creating shade

Protected spots in the garden can take many forms, from a simple patio roof, to an elaborate freestanding structure, to a grove of shade trees. We will take a look at the full range of options, all of which offer varying degrees and types of shade and protection. In addition to determining the amount of time, effort, and money you want to expend on creating a protected spot, also consider whether the shade created is for the benefit of plants, people, or both.

Left: Lath over this south-facing side garden gives shade so that houseplants can be moved outdoors during the summer. The path of white pine needles, collected from the forest, provides a natural touch. Right: This substantial stone and wood trellis supports an ancient wisteria vine and creates a perfect environment for a mass planting of ferns underneath.

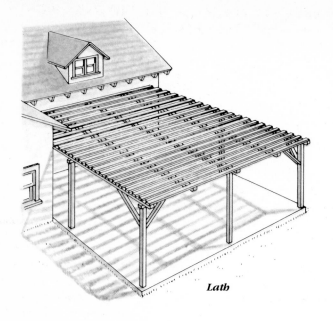

Lath

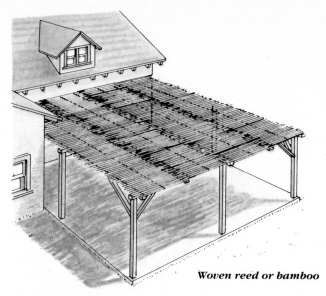

Woven reed or bamboo

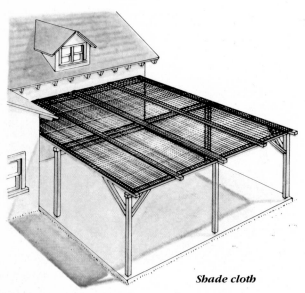

Shade cloth

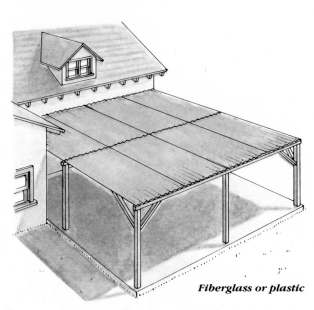

Fiberglass or plastic

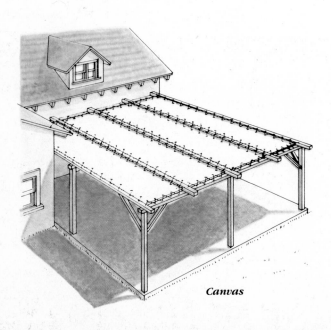

Canvas

Patio Covers

If possible, you should decide what kind of roof you want on your patio before you build the patio. Your choice of material can greatly affect the type and quality of shade you will get. You may also want to consider expense, durability, maintenance, and how easily it can be removed. Some of the advantages and disadvantages of various patio covers are discussed on the facing page.

Patio Roofs

One of the most popular shade structures is a simple patio roof. Its construction can be quick and inexpensive. Whether the roof is attached to the house or standing free, the basic framework is the same: posts, supporting beams, and rafters. The type of patio roof you choose determines how sturdy the framework must be and how far apart the rafters will be spaced.

If you want a lightweight, easy-to-install roof that admits diffused sunlight, consider plastic shade cloth over widely spaced rafters. In most climates it is more useful to soften sunlight on plants than to provide shade for people. You may have noticed shade cloth used at nurseries to shade areas for flats of seedlings or other tender plants. In its simplest form it looks like colored window screening. Available in several densities, it cuts out about half to three-quarters of the sunlight. Sometimes the nursery or garden supply store that sells it can tape edges and install grommets to your specifications. Or you can secure it with wood battens. Leave a slight sag to allow for some shrinkage. Advantages are durability, light weight, and low cost. A special advantage, if you want only a seasonal roof, is that shade cloth can be easily removed and stored.

Other patio roofs that are easy to remove from rafters and to store are woven reed and woven bamboo. They look more natural than shade cloth and cast an attractive mottled shade. Like shade cloth they are relatively inexpensive. Woven reed lasts up to four years and bamboo five years or longer, if bound by wire rather than cord.

Also removable is canvas, many people's favorite patio roof for its attractive looks and easy adaptability to many styles. A disadvantage for plants is the fact that it blocks out direct sunlight, and a disadvantage for both plants and people is the reduced air circulation. However, you can devise a design that allows the canvas to function like a window shade, opening and closing easily. Other designs also permit the free flow of air. Canvas is one of the least durable materials, but is fairly inexpensive and one of the simplest to replace.

Fiberglass and plastic panels are other inexpensive materials for roofing a patio, but they aren't easily removed for seasonal storage. An advantage that they share with canvas is providing privacy from overhead windows, especially desirable in an urban garden. Unlike canvas, they admit light and heat. In fact, they trap heat and create a greenhouse effect. By the same token, however, they are a poor choice for a hot south- or west-facing patio, as they gather too much heat and inhibit air circulation.

Wood, in various forms, is the most popular covering for outdoor living areas, largely because it permits air circulation. It can be relatively inexpensive—lath, lat-

A shaded entrance to a private world, the old-fashioned arbor and garden gate are more than just a quaint reminder of the past. Any barrier, especially a tall one, creates a division of space. In this case, the gate and arbor are symbolic: what is in front of them is what the public sees; those who pass through the gate enter the private world of the front garden. The wooden arbor, which would be overwhelming if it were constructed of stone or brick, functions solely as a support for the massive climbing rose.

tice, and grapestakes; or moderately to quite expensive—wooden overhead structures whose size and spacing can vary considerably. If you choose wooden overheads (often 2 × 3s or 1 × 2s, laid on edge), remember that not only their spacing but also the direction they are laid determines how much shade they create. For most shade plants, the lath should always be laid north-south so the bars of sunlight move across the plants. Sunlight from lath that is laid east-west moves slowly and can scorch many delicate plants.

Instead of making a patio roof entirely of wood, give some thought to minimizing the wooden structure and planting vines to cover it entirely or partially. But be sure the structure is strong enough to support the weight of a rain-dampened vine in full leaf. Some vines are fast-growing and provide shade within a season. Vines are discussed at some length later in this chapter.

Garden Structures

Shade structures in the garden are nothing new. Mesopotamian pergolas and Egyptian, Persian, and Oriental pavilions offer evidence that structures have been a part of gardens for as long as people have gardened. Many names, some synonymous and some overlapping, designate shade structures: pergola, gazebo, belvedere, summer house, pavilion, garden house, ramada, lath house, casino, and arbor. To minimize the confusion, and offer a little historical perspective on the subject, we have illustrated many different styles of garden structures below.

Shade structures can be roofed over solidly or covered just enough to diffuse direct sunlight. They can be elaborate garden living rooms or simple sheltered nooks. Their style can match or blend with the style of any house or garden. Most are built as separate, freestanding structures, but they can also be built to take advantage of an existing wall or fence.

More elaborate structures to create shade can be covered or enclosed with the same materials used for patio roofs. In addition to esthetics, other considerations become even more important when you are planning not just a roof but a structure whose sides may also be enclosed. How much air circulation do you need? Do you want to create maximum privacy? Do you want year-round shade or only summer shade? Thoughtful choice of design and materials is important.

The *pergola,* or covered walkway, dates back to the first known gardens. Pergolas are traditionally constructed using pillars, often substantial, and beams and rafters, with the addition of vines, which may envelop or merely soften and decorate the structure. A spacious, large-scale pergola may have benches or seats. In a hot-summer climate it can enable you to move about the garden comfortably, even at midday. It can also provide shelter for shade plants in hanging planters, or in containers or beds close to its north or east edge.

An *arbor* is essentially like a pergola, except that it exists for its own sake, rather than as a covering for a walkway. It is a shaded bower created by wood and vines. Trellises are sometimes a component. Its design is often simple, even rustic. This structure is probably known best as a support for grapevines.

The *lath house,* usually freestanding but often attached to the house, is more often designed to provide shade for plants than for people, although you can make a wonderfully comfortable living area by situating garden furniture among its fuchsias, tuberous begonias, and ferns. For maximum privacy let vines cover areas of lath wall, but be careful not to cut out too much air circulation and light.

When most people think of freestanding shade structures in the garden, they think of garden houses, by whatever name—*gazebo,* for example. Some of the most graceful were built in the gardens of colonial Williamsburg. Some of the less graceful were constructed of heavy iron during the Victorian era. A traditional garden house of the Southwest is the *ramada,* a roughhewn structure of heavy log posts and beams covered by poles or by

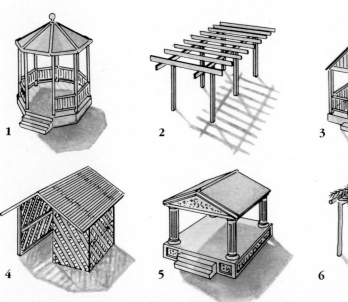

Shade Structures
1. *Gazebo or belvedere*
2. *Pergola or arbor*
3. *Summer house or garden house*
4. *Lath house*
5. *Casino or Roman summer house*
6. *Ramada*

palm leaves, reeds, or yucca stalks. Whatever the style of your house and garden, a garden house can be built in the same style, or in a simple modern design that blends in well.

Your garden house can have a floor of wood, concrete, stone, brick, tiles, or gravel (although gravel is practical only if seats are stationary). Attractive flooring can be made with wooden rounds, stone, or brick, with gaps filled by a low ground cover, such as Corsican mint (*Mentha requienii*), if there is enough light and moisture.

If you live in an area where mosquitoes, flies, or gnats are a problem, consider screening in your garden house. To increase the versatility of your structure, you might install folding louvered panels. Plants in containers or hanging baskets are an attractive embellishment and a link with the garden. Even the simplest garden house might be wired to permit the use of electric fans, lights, and music.

Your garden house can serve multiple functions. For example, it can include outdoor cooking and dining facilities, or an attractively enclosed tool shed and potting area. It can house a hot tub, and part or all of it can serve as a dressing room near the pool or hot tub. You can design a garden house that serves as a simple shelter from the sun and a vantage point for viewing the garden, or a shelter that provides in addition most of the comforts of a home-across-the-garden.

Whatever kind of shade structure you decide on, consider calling in an architect or a landscape architect for consultation and maybe for the design itself. A professional has the knowledge to help you avoid costly, unfortunate mistakes and to create the structure that will best suit your needs.

Left: In the Old Westbury Gardens in New York, elaborate gazebos and arbors in the Chinese style form the architectural backdrop of a formal perennial garden. Below: Also in the Old Westbury Gardens, a walkway is enhanced by a substantial pergola which is covered with ivy and climbing roses.

Vines for Shade

You have probably already begun to think about how vines might be used to soften your garden structure and create more shade. Vines also add their own individual beauty to the garden. Many flower, and some have fragrant flowers. A few produce edible fruit. All can shelter an area from the wind and make it more private. All can mask a harsh wall or a graceless structure. Most are fast growers that provide shade and other benefits far faster than most trees.

Following are two lists: first, deciduous and annual vines, then evergreen vines, with brief descriptions and enough information to let you decide which vines would be right for your shade structure. The obvious advantages of an evergreen vine, particularly in a mild climate where the garden is used much of the year, are permanent greenery, privacy, and shelter from wind and sun. Not surprisingly, most evergreen vines are hardy only in the warmer zones. A deciduous or annual vine, on the other hand, creates a pleasant sense of seasonal change and sometimes provides brilliant autumn color. And even more important, it admits light in winter and makes shade in summer.

Whatever vine you choose, follow these guidelines: Don't buy a root-bound vine that has been too long in its nursery can. Plant the vine in the same way you would plant a shrub or a tree, but dig an especially deep and wide hole—even 3 feet by 3 feet, if possible. Fertilize and water regularly, and prune to shape the vine and control its spreading.

Deciduous Vines.   Here are some of the best deciduous vines for shade structures:

Actinidia chinensis (Chinese Gooseberry, Kiwi Vine; Hardy to Zone 8) grows rapidly to 30 feet, forming woody stems. This vine climbs by twining, and should be tied to a structure. The 2-inch creamy flowers, which appear in early summer, are fragrant and moderately showy. The 3 to 6-inch leaves, dark green on top, whitish beneath, make deep shade. It is valued for its foliage and delicious fruit; both a female and a male vine are necessary for fruiting. Plant in light shade to full sun, and protect from strong winds. Chinese gooseberry bears on last year's wood, so leave plenty of it when you prune in early spring.

Campsis × *tagliabuana* 'Mme. Galen' ('Mme. Galen' Trumpet Vine; Hardy to Zone 5) is a rapid grower that reaches a height of 30 feet. It attaches to wood or masonry, but should be held by wire or other support once it gets heavy. Salmon-red 2½-inch flowers bloom in showy clusters from July to September. The coarse-textured, glossy leaves are compound, each leaflet 2 inches long. For best blooming, plant in full sun. It blooms on new growth, so prune in early spring. Many other members of this genus can work well. Check with your local nursery.

Clematis hybrids (Clematis; Hardiness varies) grow fast to 15 feet. These vines twine but often need tying. They sport spectacular summer blossoms to 6 inches wide. The leaves are small, their stems twining about supports. Most hybrids bloom on the current season's

growth, so prune in early spring. Clematis often looks twiggy, spindly, and dead in the winter. This is not a good choice to cover large areas. Its roots require cool, rich, slightly alkaline soil. Plant deep, with the roots in shade and the top in light shade to full sun.

Gourds are annuals. Plant seeds 18 inches apart in full sun, when the ground has warmed. The vines climb by tendrils. With adequate summer heat over several months, vines grow fast to 20 or 30 feet and bear well. Most have yellow flowers and large, luxuriant leaves. Gourds vary greatly in size, color, shape, and texture. Plant in full sun, and protect them from strong wind.

Ipomoea tricolor (Morning Glory) is an annual that grows quickly to 15 feet and climbs by twining. The 5-inch flowers (various colors) appear from late spring to frost. The leaves are dark green and heart-shaped. Plant in full sun.

Parthenocissus quinquefolia (Virginia Creeper; Hardy to Zone 4), after a slow start, grows rapidly to 50 feet. It climbs by tendril "suckers" that attach to any surface. Flowers and fruit are inconspicuous. This vine is valued for its five-sectioned leaves, which grow to 6 inches wide, bright green in spring and summer, and brilliant red in fall. When the woody stems are bare in winter, their tracery on a wall is attractive. Plant in light shade to full sun. Its relative, *Parthenocissus tricuspidata* (Boston Ivy; Hardy to Zone 5), is the same in nearly every respect except that its leaves are not lobed.

Polygonum aubertii (Silverlace Vine; Hardy to Zone 5) grows quickly to 30 feet or more, climbing by twining stems. The flowers are whitish, in dense, heavy clusters, from spring into fall. These are its great asset. The leaves are heart-shaped, light green, to 2 inches long. Plant in full sun. This vine can be pruned to the ground annually, in the fall. This is an exceptionally tough, care-free, heat-tolerant plant that grows in nearly any soil.

The many species and varieties of *Rosa* (Climbing Roses) grow quickly to 10 to 30 feet. Their hardiness varies according to species. Roses need to be tied firmly or woven into a supporting structure. They need full sun, good soil, air circulation, and often the same spraying that bush roses need. Plant in full sun. Thin and prune out dead wood and crossing branches early in spring.

Vitis species and varieties (Grapes) have been cultivated throughout history. Their hardiness varies according to species. Some are mainly ornamental, while others produce table and wine grapes. All climb by tendrils. Their stems are large and woody, growth fast to variable. Flowers are inconspicuous, but the large, roundish, lobed leaves are always beautiful. Plant in full sun. Prune heavily in spring for fruiting. For ornamental use, prune lightly to shape. Check with your nursery or county agent for the best varieties for your area.

Left: The fall color of Boston ivy is spectacular. Leaves are bright green throughout the spring and summer. Top right: The climbing rose 'American Pillar'. Bottom right: Fragrant spring blossoms of wisteria are an all-time favorite in many gardens.

Wisteria floribunda (Japanese Wisteria; Hardy to Zone 5), once established, climbs rapidly to 25 or 30 feet by twining. The stems become woody and heavy with age. Fragrant blue-violet flowers hang in clusters 12 to 40 inches in length. White, purple, and rose forms are also available. The 16-inch leaves, divided into many leaflets, turn yellow in fall. Plant in full sun. Prune and thin immediately after flowering, or in winter. Encourage blooming by supplementing fertilizer in spring with superphosphate. This species is hardier than *W. sinensis* (Chinese Wisteria), which has shorter, denser flower clusters.

Evergreen Vines. Among the great number of evergreen vines, here are a few of the best for shade structures:

Bougainvillea species and varieties (Bougainvillea; Hardy in Zone 10), once established, are fast growing to 15 to 25 feet. Bougainvillea needs sturdy supports and tying, despite its hooked spines and twining stems. Its "flowers" are actually bracts, appearing over the entire plant spring through fall. Varieties range from scarlet and magenta to orange-yellow and white. Leaves are 2 to 3 inches in length, and dense. Prune heavily in spring, thinning the vine and removing canes from the base. The roots are very fussy, so disturb them as little as possible. Good drainage and the sunniest, hottest spot in the garden are required.

Clematis armandii (Evergreen Clematis; Hardy to Zone 8) grows slowly at first, then quickly to 15 to 20 feet. It climbs by tendrils but benefits from tying onto a sturdy support. Masses of very fragrant, creamy, 2-inch flowers appear in spring. The plumelike seed structures are decorative in late summer. The 6-inch leaves come in threes and are scythe-shaped and glossy dark green. They create an attractive texture. Plant in light shade or in full sun with roots in shade. Prune imme-

diately after flowering to thin and encourage new growth. Evergreen clematis is particularly attractive on eaves, fence tops, arbors, and pergolas.

Distictis buccinatoria, formerly called *Bignonia cherere* (Blood-Red Trumpet Vine), grows slowly at first, then quickly to 30 feet. It climbs by tendrils that form strong disks, which are sometimes damaging to wood. It needs firm support. The 4-inch trumpet flowers, marked with gold inside and at the base, bloom in large clusters from May to November. Flowers open brick red, fading to purplish red. The leaves grow to 3 inches long, and are dark green and dense. Plant in partial shade or full sun. Prune in spring to remove weak stems and prevent matting.

Gelsemium sempervirens (Carolina Jessamine; Hardy to Zone 8) grows at a moderate rate to 20 to 30 feet. It climbs by twining, and needs sturdy support. Masses of buttery yellow, fragrant tubular flowers, 1½ inches long, begin blooming in the late winter or early spring, and last for 2 to 4 months. The dense, attractive, glossy green leaves grow to 3 inches long. Plant in sun or partial shade. Prune to thin the vine just after blooming. Every part of this plant is extremely poisonous to eat but safe to touch.

Hedera helix (English Ivy; Hardy to Zone 6) grows moderately or quickly to 50 feet or higher. It climbs by roots that attach firmly to wood, concrete, or stone. The dark green leaves are lobed, 2 to 4 inches long. The vine forms dense woody mats. Because it can damage wood and is an aggressive grower, out into the garden as well as onto structures, it is not a choice plant for shade structures. Its hardiness is its chief value. Plant in shade or partial shade, or sun in cool areas. Prune vigorously at any time. Many varieties are available.

Jasminum polyanthum (Bridal Jasmine) grows quickly to 20 or 30 feet. It climbs by twining, and may benefit from weaving through structures or tying. Dense clusters of deep-rose buds open white and very fragrant in the spring and summer, or periodically throughout the year in warmest zones. The leaves, finely divided into five to seven leaflets, are handsome year-round. Plant in medium shade to full sun. Thin and shape yearly, after flowering. Many other species of flowering jasmine are available regionally.

Lonicera hildebrandiana (Burmese Honeysuckle; Hardy to Zone 9) is fast growing to 20 feet or more. It is slightly twining, but does best tied or woven onto a firm support. The highly fragrant 7-inch tubular flowers open white, aging to gold or bronze, throughout summer. The 6-inch, glossy dark leaves are beautiful year-round. Plant in sun, or partial shade in hottest areas. Thin and shape after blooming. Many other species of honeysuckle are regionally available, some quite hardy.

Left: The beautiful yellow flowers of the Carolina jessamine are fragrant and last for two to four months. The vine is evergreen, needs sturdy support, and climbs by twining. Right: Its delicate white flowers make star jasmine among the most sweetly fragrant of all flowering vines.

Passiflora caerulea (Bluecrown Passionflower; Hardy to Zone 8) is semievergreen in colder areas. It grows rampantly to 20 or 30 feet, attaching itself by tendrils. It does best on a strong lattice. Its fascinatingly complicated 3 to 4-inch flowers bloom in white, pinkish, or bluish purple throughout the summer. Leaves are five-lobed, blue-green above and gray-green beneath. Plant in full sun. If not pruned often and severely, it forms a heavy mat. Many less hardy tropical species are available in warmest areas.

Rosa banksiae (Lady Banks' Rose; Hardy to Zone 8) has evergreen, nearly thornless branches that grow fast to 20 to 30 feet, requiring sturdy support and some tying. In coldest winters it drops leaves. Unlike most roses, this one is virtually disease-free. Its small double flowers bloom in large clusters from spring into summer. Both a yellow and a white form are available. The white form ('Alba Plena') is fragrant. The glossy, dark-green leaflets grow to 2 inches. Plant in full sun or light shade. Prune in early spring.

Trachelospermum jasminoides (Star Jasmine, Confederate Jasmine; Hardy to Zone 9) grows slowly at first, to 10 to 20 feet. It climbs by twining, and needs weaving or tying to a supporting structure. The small white flowers bloom in fragrant clusters in the late spring and summer. The waxy, dark green, 2 to 3-inch leaves are exceptionally attractive. Star jasmine takes full sun anywhere. Little pruning is needed, but prune to shape in fall. In hot areas, plant in some shade.

Shade Trees

Few people would disagree that trees provide the best and most beautiful shade of all, but not everyone has the patience to wait for a small shade tree to mature. If there are already mature shade trees in your garden, count your blessings. It's much easier to modify existing trees to meet your needs than it is to produce shade overnight.

Aside from having to wait for a tree to produce its desired effect, there are advantages to planting your own shade trees. Most important, you can be assured of having exactly what you want—the right size and kind of tree, deciduous, evergreen, flowering, or fruiting—and you can place it where it will provide the most benefit. The following pages are designed to assist you in the selection of the right tree. As most gardeners want maximum openness and brightness in winter and early spring, there are more deciduous than evergreen trees in the lists that follow. Since the purpose of these lists is to suggest trees for shading gardens, most of the trees described branch high, or can be easily pruned to do so, leaving ample room for gardening beneath them.

Since most modern gardens are small and trees often grow close to the pavement, foundations, and drainpipes, the majority of these trees have deep roots, if properly watered from the start. Most of them are reasonably clean. There is also a separate list of small-scale shade trees, most of which are adaptable to large containers in a terrace garden. Neither list is by any means

exhaustive. For more details and selection, consult the Ortho book *The World of Trees*. Here are suggestions for some of the all-around best shade trees, to help you see what is possible as you begin to choose trees for your garden.

Ginkgo biloba (Ginkgo or Maidenhair Tree; Hardy to Zone 5) is deciduous. Its growth rate is variable but usually slow to 60 to 100 feet; it may grow 10 feet in 9 years. Usually conical in youth, it becomes open and wide-spreading as it ages, so that its shade is broken, not deep. It has no significant pests or diseases, and is tolerant of pollution. The fan-shaped leaves turn brilliant gold all at once, then fall quickly. This ancient tree dates back to the Jurassic period.

Gleditsia triacanthos inermis 'Sunburst' ('Sunburst' Honey Locust; Hardy to Zone 5) is deciduous, and grows quickly to 35 to 50 feet. It is upright and spreading, forming a vase shape. It leafs out late and drops leaves early, making very light shade. It is tolerant of pollution and heat. The leaves are finely divided and golden, creating a lacy appearance; green forms are also available.

Liriodendron tulipifera (Tulip Tree; Hardy to Zone 5) is a deciduous tree, fast-growing to 70 feet or taller in a tall, pyramidal form. Its handsome, squarish, medium-green leaves make medium shade and soft-yellow autumn color. The flowers are beautiful but concealed in foliage. George Washington framed his view at Mount Vernon with a pair of tulip trees. Roots can be dense near the surface, so the tree needs deep watering; it is not drought-tolerant.

Metasequoia glyptostroboides (Dawn Redwood; Hardy to Zone 6) is a deciduous conifer. It grows quickly to 75 feet or higher, growing 35 feet in 10 years. It has a pyramidal form, and makes medium shade. Its bare form is beautiful in winter. Despite the great size of adult trees, the young tree is suitable for planter culture. Like the ginkgo this is an ancient tree, but rather new to American gardens.

Pinus thunbergiana (Japanese Black Pine; Hardy to Zone 5) grows quickly to 90 feet, much slower and smaller (but healthy) in hot, dry climates. It has a picturesque, irregular habit, and is very malleable—it can be pruned to any shape and kept at the desired size, even as a bonsai. The degree of shade it gives depends on shaping.

Pistacia chinensis (Chinese Pistache; Hardy to Zone 9) is deciduous, with a moderate growth rate to 50 to 60 feet and as wide. Its graceful, finely divided leaves make filtered shade and spectacular tones of red, orange, and yellow in fall. It has a short trunk and a zigzag branching pattern. It needs staking and shaping when very young. It has no particular pests or diseases, and thrives in wide range of climates, including extreme heat.

Chinese pistache (Pistacia chinensis) is one of the most valuable shade trees to plant in a lawn or along a street. The shade it casts when mature is light enough to allow a healthy lawn or other planting to grow beneath it, and its leaves are so small that they hardly need to be raked.

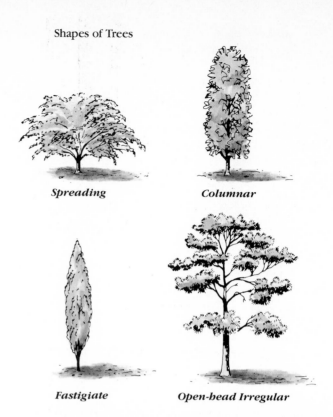

Shapes of Trees

Spreading *Columnar*

Fastigiate *Open-head Irregular*

Cone

Globe

Weeping

Smaller Trees

Besides the trees described below, consider *Acer palmatum, Acer circinatum, Cercis canadensis,* and appropriate *Cornus* species, all discussed in the *Plant Selection Guide* as small trees suitable for use beneath a canopy of tall trees. In milder climates all will grow in full sun.

The fringe tree (Chionanthus virginicus) is one of the most beautiful of all woodland plants. Masses of fragrant white flowers cover the tree in the late spring, and the foliage turns golden in fall. Plants grow easily in the medium shade beneath this tree.

Quercus robur 'Fastigiata' (Pyramidal English Oak; Hardy to Zone 6) is a deciduous tree with a moderate to fast growth rate to 70 feet or higher. Its habit is columnar in youth, pyramidal in maturity. The lobed leaves make medium shade, and hang on until late in the season. Many other oaks, both deciduous and evergreen, are available regionally.

Robinia pseudoacacia (Black Locust; Hardy to Zone 4) is deciduous, with a fast growth rate to 40 to 75 feet. Its umbrellalike form, sparse and open, casts very light shade. Long, hanging clusters of fragrant white flowers appear in late spring among divided leaves. Although it is subject to some pests, this is one of the toughest trees, thriving in the poorest soils, under adverse conditions, and with complete neglect.

Sophora japonica (Japanese Pagoda Tree; Chinese Scholar Tree; Hardy to Zone 5) is deciduous, with a slow growth rate to 20 or 30 feet, then a moderate rate to 50 to 75 feet and as wide. Its dense, upright form in youth rounds and spreads with age. The large, lustrous, dark green leaves, divided into many leaflets, turn yellow in autumn. Clouds of white, wisterialike flowers bloom in late summer. Flowers and pods can litter walks and patios.

Zelkova serrata (Sawleaf or Japanese Zelkova; Hardy to Zone 6) is deciduous, with a moderate to fast growth to 50 or 60 feet and as wide. It is roundish as a young tree, vase-shaped as an older tree. The leaves are oval and serrated, very similar to those of the closely related American elm. It makes medium shade. Unlike the elm it is disease and pest-resistant, and the roots are not often bothersome, particularly with deep watering. Young trees need pruning to establish a proper framework.

Chionanthus virginicus (Fringe Tree; Hardy to Zone 5) is deciduous, with a slow growth rate to 20 to 30 feet. Its large, bold leaves and open form cast medium shade. Leaves appear very late in spring, and turn golden in fall. The masses of small, fragrant, white flowers that appear in late spring are among the most beautiful flowers of any woodland plant. Dark blue berries appear in fall. Fringe tree will remain multitrunked and shrubby unless pruned to single trunk.

Cladrastis lutea (Yellowwood; Hardy to Zone 4) is deciduous, with a slow growth rate to 30 to 35 feet. Its upright branches create a vase shape. The large leaves, divided into leaflets, turn yellow in fall. The dense foliage makes medium shade. Beautiful, intensely fragrant wisterialike flowers cover the mature tree in June, and the branches and pods are attractive in winter. This is a tough tree, one that will withstand drought, extremes of temperature, and wet or alkaline soils.

Crataegus laevigata 'Paulii', also sold as *C. oxyacantha* 'Paul's Scarlet' ('Paul's Scarlet' English Hawthorn; Hardy to Zone 5) is a deciduous tree with a moderate growth rate to 20 to 25 feet. Of the many hawthorns, this is perhaps the most beautiful for its masses of double, intensely rose-red flowers in late May, followed by sprinkling of ½-inch scarlet berries in fall. The lobed, dense foliage makes medium shade. The tree forms a spreading, roundish crown. It is susceptible to fireblight; check with your local nursery to find out whether another hawthorn is better suited to your area.

Franklinia alatamaha (Franklinia; Hardy to Zone 6) is deciduous, with a slow to moderate growth to 20 to 30 feet. The tree forms an upright, open pyramid. Its glossy leaves grow to 6 inches long, loose and open, and cast light to medium shade. The striking 3-inch flowers, which resemble single white camellias or roses, appear in fall, often as the foliage turns brilliant orangered. This tree prefers some shade in hottest areas. It is perfect for the woodland garden, beneath a canopy of taller trees.

Koelreuteria paniculata (Goldenrain Tree; Hardy to Zone 6) is deciduous, with a moderate to fast growth to 30 feet. This tree is rounded when young, flat-topped at maturity. The open branches and bold-textured, compound leaves cast medium shade. Large clusters of bright yellow flowers cover the tree in early or midsummer, followed by fruits like Chinese lanterns, which remain through fall. It is tolerant of most adverse conditions.

Laburnum watereri 'Vossii' (Golden-Chain Tree; Vossii Laburnum; Hardy to Zone 6) is deciduous, with a moderate rate of growth to 20 to 30 feet. This upright, vase-shaped tree should be pruned to a single trunk. The bright green leaves are divided into three leaflets. It makes light to medium shade, and in hot climates prefers to grow in a little shade. In May, 18-inch pendant clusters of buttery yellow, wisterialike flowers appear. All parts are poisonous to eat but not to touch.

Magnolia soulangiana (Saucer Magnolia; Hardy to Zone 6) is a deciduous tree with a moderate growth rate to 25 feet. There is a great deal of variation in habit, flower color, and size among the many varieties, but the species is spreading and open. It can be pruned early as a single-trunked tree, or allowed to spread wide as a multitrunked tree. The leaves are 8 inches long, fairly dense, and make medium shade. The large (5 to 10 inches), spectacular, cup-shaped flowers appear before the foliage, even during winter in mildest areas. The species has white to rosy-red flowers, while varieties have white, purple, pink, or delicately tinted flowers. The tree blooms while still quite young. If you live in an area of late frost, ask at your local nursery about late-blooming varieties.

Malus floribunda (Japanese Flowering Crabapple; Hardy to Zone 5) is a deciduous favorite among over 600 species and varieties of crabapple. It has a medium to fast growth rate to 20 to 30 feet. Its spreading, gracefully arching growth casts medium shade. Masses of rosy buds open into pinkish flowers that fade to white. Ornamental reddish yellow ⅜-inch fruit appears in late summer, borne dependably if there has been some winter chilling; the fruit attracts birds.

Maytenus boaria (Mayten; Hardy to Zone 9) is an evergreen with a slow growth rate to 35 feet or higher, although it is usually seen as a smaller tree. It becomes rounded, with gracefully pendulous branchlets and dainty, glossy leaves. It casts light to medium shade. Flowers and fruit are tiny and inconspicuous. This is one of the choicest small evergreen trees for mild-winter areas.

The rosy blossoms that cover the Japanese flowering crabapple are a signal that spring has arrived.

Modifying shade

Shade is a desirable element in the garden only up to a point. If your garden feels dark and dank because it is too heavily shaded by overgrown trees, you will want to prune them back so that you will have full use of your space. If you have moved into a home with an older, neglected garden it will probably be worth your while to hire professionals to do the pruning. The cost of such extensive work is usually considerable, but the results can be dramatic or even shocking if you are unfamiliar with the great ability of plants to renew themselves quickly. An additional benefit to having overgrown trees and shrubs professionally pruned is that most companies will either haul the debris away as part of the total cost, or bring a chipper to the site, leaving the material for use as a mulch or for compost.

If you have only a few problem trees, the information on pruning in this chapter will help you make the right cuts. You'll need a good pruning saw, the type with a curved blade on the end of an extension pole, a wide-bladed saw similar to a carpenter's saw, and a pair of hand pruners.

Increasing Light

A mature tree casts dense shade, limiting the selection of plants that will grow beneath it.

Selective thinning creates dappled shade, and permits a wider selection.

In addition to producing too much shade, mature trees pose other problems for the gardener who would like to make good use of the ground beneath their spreading branches. Depending on the type of tree, the soil directly around mature specimens is often congested with roots, leaving little space for other plants to grow. An overly dense canopy of leaves can also severely restrict air circulation, an important element for the healthy growth of plants. Mature trees have prodigious appetites when it comes to nutrients and water. This fact must be taken into consideration before planting smaller plants, whose root systems may not be able to compete with those of the larger tree.

If the shade in your yard is not produced by trees, but by neighboring structures, there are fewer options in modifying the conditions. Painting the walls a light color will help to reflect whatever available light there is, and can often make a significant difference in the mood of the garden. Beyond that solution, the best advice is to make your plant selections carefully according to the prevailing conditions and follow the instructions on page 27 for improving the soil.

Pruning for More Light

There are two basic methods of pruning, *thinning* and *heading back,* both of which are usually necessary at some time in the life of a tree. Thinning means to take out whole branches, and produces a more open, graceful-looking specimen. Thinning is the most important type of pruning you can do if your objective is to permit more light to reach the ground and to increase air circulation. Before pruning any branches, examine the tree and the shade pattern it casts at various times throughout the day. When thinning a shade tree, first remove any rubbing branches, or those that grow toward the center of the tree rather than outward. Never remove more than a third of the branches a year. Trees respond to severe pruning with a rush of vigorous growth which can choke the tree and make it more dense than ever. If you wish to prune heavily, do so in late June or July, when this vigorous response will be less.

If less shade is desired after these branches are removed, selectively prune away small branches before removing a major limb. Continue pruning one branch at a time until the desired amount of shade is left. No matter what size branch you are pruning, always prune at a junction of two branches, and cut flush, never leaving a stub.

Heading back involves removing the ends of the branches to create denser foliage and a bushier plant. If only part of a limb is pruned off, this practice does not reduce shade, except around the periphery of the plant; it does help create a more dense shade. The same rules that apply to thinning, in terms of cutting and amount to prune, apply to heading back.

There are some cases where the garden would benefit from the complete removal of a large shrub or tree. If the plants were placed too close to begin with, the

Selectively pruned trees allow enough light for underplanting with colorful beds of annuals or perennials, or shrubs.

passage of time only makes the situation worse. When deciding which plant has to go, spend some time imagining what the area will look like in its absence. If possible, have someone pull the plant as far to one side as it can go while you stand back and make a choice. This is a cautious first step that can take some of the worry out of an irrevocable decision.

Minimizing Root Competition

Some trees, such as maples and elms, naturally produce a great mass of surface roots. Other trees that are normally deep-rooting will often produce quantities of surface roots when planted in a garden situation merely to take advantage of the frequent, shallow irrigations from sprinklers. In either case, too many roots in a planting area beneath trees causes problems for smaller plants. Often the competition for nutrients and water is so rigorous that the smaller plant either dies or simply never grows. Here are some ways to deal with this.

Choose plants that compete well with the tree roots. Your local nursery people can advise you on these choices. A watering and feeding system that places the water and nutrients directly to the area around these plants is another obvious way to help them compete.

Root pruning outside the drip line of the tree can also help. This is done by digging a 16 to 18-inch trench, cutting and clearing the planting area of tree roots. After this is done once, it's easier in subsequent years. If you lay a sheet of black plastic against the side of the trench as a further deterrent to invading tree roots, you may be able to skip a year or two.

It's important to remember that as you improve the soil for the plants you are adding, you are also encouraging the tree roots to grow into that area.

If all you really desire is a little color under an aging shade tree, and the previous suggestions sound like too

CREATING AND MODIFYING SHADE

Decreasing Root Competition

Plastic or metal root barrier

New shrubs

Root pruning and the addition of a barrier to hold new root growth back will help keep competition under control.

Increasing Air Circulation

An overgrown and neglected shrub limits air circulation to the surrounding plants.

Pruning to raise the canopy and eliminate tangled branches not only permits more air and light but also usually makes the shrub more attractive.

much work, there's yet another solution. You can build a simple portable deck, and place containers of colorful, shade-loving annuals on top of it. This can be especially useful under oak trees with a susceptibility to oak root fungus. One of the major deterrents to oak root fungus is keeping the surface soil as dry as possible. With a portable deck, and a few containers, you can have your flowers and the oaks too.

Maximizing Air Circulation

Farmers are well aware of the wind-reduction properties of trees. For countless generations they have planted rows of towering trees to act as windbreaks, protecting valuable crops. In smaller gardens, however, a tree's ability to reduce wind and air circulation can have a harmful effect, especially in humid climates.

In any garden where disease is a problem, air circulation should be maximized. A large tree, dense with foliage, not only limits air circulation, but also increases the humidity of the garden by decreasing the amount of available sunlight. The lower a leafy canopy is to the ground, the more it contributes to stagnant air. For maximum air circulation, trees should be pruned as high off the ground as possible without detracting from the esthetics of the garden. The thinning process (see page 43) will also help increase circulation.

Limiting the number of plants in the garden and giving them plenty of space to grow will also help minimize disease problems. If diseases such as powdery mildew, rust, and mold are still a yearly occurrence, you should use a commercial fungicide. Fungicides are best used as a deterrent to disease rather than as a cure. For that reason, they should be applied *before* the problem occurs in any given year, or at the very first sign of attack, to limit the damage. Consult your nursery for product names and best times for application.

CREATING GARDENS IN THE SHADE

Do you want a subtle, sophisticated shade garden? A cool retreat? Or a cheerful, colorful corner to glimpse from the kitchen window? Do you prefer a formal or a natural style? Here's the information to help you decide.

All successful gardens, no matter what their location or exposure, are a combination of three things: the sensitive use of plants for color, texture, and foliage; a well-thought-out plan or design; and more often than not, the employing of a *style* to pull the whole scene together. This chapter takes a look at all three areas, with special attention to the process of selecting and combining plants in the shade garden.

People with shaded garden areas often feel that their selection of plants is so limited that only the most common sort of garden can be created. Although gardeners do have fewer plant choices for shade than for sunny conditions, the list of possibilities is extensive enough to create a sophisticated and interesting garden.

The importance of plant selection

Two points make creating a shade garden different from creating a garden in the sun: There are fewer plants to choose from; and there are fewer plants that produce bright color. Not only is there a smaller "vocabulary" of plant material, but shade gardeners have to make that material mean more than it normally does in other gardens, where the focus is on splashy, sun-loving plants. In short, shade gardeners have to create more, with less.

The problem in providing color in the shade comes not so much from the limited number of plants that will bloom in the shade (there are literally hundreds of choices) but from the type of color they provide. Gardeners used to the dramatic seasonal displays of sun-

Left: A superb example of a woodland garden. Hostas, ajuga, azaleas, rhododendrons, ferns, jack-in-the-pulpit, and Solomon's seal thrive in the filtered light produced by towering trees. Right: A more restrained interpretation of a woodland garden features a well-groomed lawn, azaleas, rhododendrons, dwarf spruce, juniper, and bleeding heart. In both cases, the owners of the gardens made the most of the conditions offered them.

loving petunias, marigolds, zinnias, and other popular annuals may find it hard to adjust to the more demure, less powerful blossoms of most shade-loving plants. But good shade gardeners are both smart and sensitive. They have found out by experimentation and observation that there are many attractive ways around the most perplexing limitations. For specific information about selecting the most effective plants for your area, see *Color in the Shade,* page 13.

Planning and designing a garden

Unfortunately, the planning stage is often ignored by beginning gardeners. Most gardens grow willy-nilly by bits and pieces, and if some overall design eventually does emerge it is more by luck than by conscious effort. Most gardeners are faced with one of two situations: renovating an existing garden planted by a former owner, or creating a new garden from scratch surrounding a new home. In either case the temptation is to hurry off to the nursery or garden center to buy a few plants for immediate results. In the long run, however, you will create a more beautiful garden if you take the time to draw up an overall plan.

Chances are that any garden that catches your eye had the benefit of a carefully designed plan early in its life. The shape and size of the lawn, the paths and walkways, decks, patios, and other sitting areas, shade trees, shrub borders, hedges, and garden structures were all considered both individually and in light of how each contributed to the total effect.

By the time your garden matures, the underlying structure or design may not be as apparent as when the plants were still young, but the organization it gives the garden will still be strongly felt. The sense of order a plan provides is important, particularly in gardens where a wide variety of plant material is used. With a variety of plants of different sizes, textures, shapes, colors, and forms, there is always the possibility of ending up with a jumble, or a junglelike scene. But if the "bones" of the garden are strong any combination of plants can be supported easily, without the fear of chaos taking over.

If you are unsure of your ability to design your own garden, this is the time to hire a professional landscape architect or designer. The relatively small fee charged to draw up a plan will be more than paid back during the life of the garden in terms of beauty, the lack of costly mistakes, and ease of maintenance. Once the plan has been drawn up you can also request suggestions for plant material, or make up your own list. You can do the actual construction and planting yourself, or put it out to bid by landscape contracting companies.

The first and most important step in garden design is to determine what uses the garden will serve—as an outdoor living and entertaining area for adults, a playground for children, a space to house a particular plant collection, or an area for retreat and meditation—and what will be needed to make the garden fulfill that function, once this is determined.

There are basically four steps in designing a garden:

■ Determine the point from which the garden will most often be seen.

■ Consider the shape and topography of your yard and which plants or other objects are presently in place that you cannot move or that you want to keep.

■ Decide whether you want a formal or an informal design.

■ Choose the style that you want to predominate.

The first step in planning a garden should be to determine from what angle or location the scene will most often be viewed. Planting a garden is much like painting a picture: like the artist, the gardener uses color, texture, form, and line to create something interesting to look at. If the garden will be viewed primarily from inside the house, make sure the picture through your favorite window is the one you want to see. If you spend a lot of time on the deck or patio, you'll make it even more enjoyable by laying out your garden with that spot in mind.

Next, think about the size and shape of your yard, the slope of the ground, and areas of sun and shade at various times of the year. Are there large trees that you will have to work around? Are they deciduous or evergreen? How about garden furniture—is it movable or stationary? Are there any garden structures, existing or projected? If you take all of these factors into account from the beginning, your garden will be sure to fit your needs and tastes.

Once you determine the angle from which your garden will be most often enjoyed, and identify the elements you have to work with, the next decision involves lines and shapes: will you lay out the garden on formal straight lines, or on a less formal, naturalistic design of random curves?

The decision to plan a formal or informal garden may be influenced as much by the existing conditions of your lot as by your esthetic preferences. If the topography of your yard is irregular, with slopes, hills, or rock outcroppings, or if there are a number of mature trees that you wish to leave standing, you'll find it difficult to carry out a formal design. Such a site lends itself naturally to an informal plan, and most gardeners with these conditions will be content to let them dictate the style. On the other hand, if your yard is relatively flat, with no outstanding natural features, you'll be free to choose whatever style you wish.

Formal gardens are composed primarily of straight lines and classical symmetry—that is, what appears on the right side of the garden is matched, sometimes nearly perfectly, on the left side. The outermost dimension of the garden is frequently rectangular, and this shape is repeated in other parts of the plan—in pools, patios, and flower beds and borders. Often a single object, such as a statue, pool, or sundial, is chosen as the center of interest; for optimum effect, it is usually placed toward the rear of the garden, directly in the line of sight from your favorite viewing spot. A formal design is the easiest type of garden to lay out, and, because of its visual simplicity, is the best choice for a small lot.

An informal garden features a predominance of curved flowing lines and a seeming disregard for symmetry. The curves of lawn areas, patios, walkways, beds, and borders are usually gentle, wide arcs that frequently follow the natural terrain. One curve should lead to another, creating a feeling of natural harmony.

A Plan for Shade
This well-designed garden makes use of various kinds of shade (see page 8), but it also retains some sunny areas. 1. Lawn areas. 2. Garage. 3. Fenced utility area. 4. Driveway. 5. Covered patio. 6. Vegetable garden in sunniest spot. 7. Large tree for summer cooling on south side of house. 8. Naturalistic pathway leading from sidewalk through a densely shaded area. 9. Clumps of tall trees for privacy. 10. Trees to create shaded seating area for viewing the house and garden.

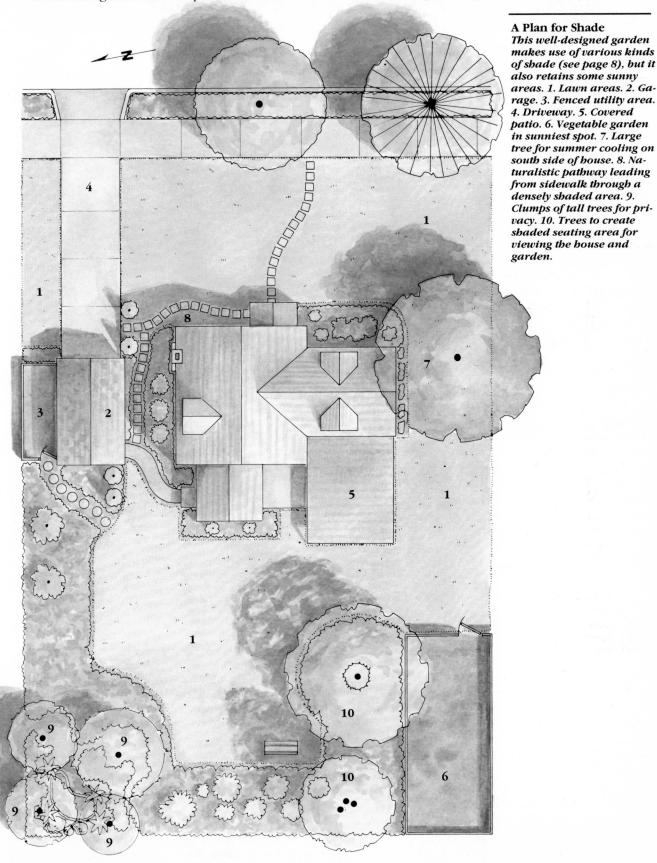

CREATING GARDENS IN THE SHADE

Garden styles

Styles of gardening are slow to develop. Generations of gardeners experiment with plants, their cultural requirements and growing conditions, and with garden designs. What is handed down from one gardener to the next are the successes—"styles" of gardening that succeed for two important reasons: they are esthetically pleasing, and they permit the desired plants not just to grow, but to flourish. A shade garden in the Japanese style, for example, is not only beautiful to look at, but if properly pulled together provides an ideal environment for ferns, mosses, azaleas, and other characteristic plants.

On pages 50 to 55 two distinct styles of gardens are examined. These styles—woodland and oriental gardens—are particularly well-suited to the use of shade-loving plants. Neither of these styles may appeal to your personal taste, or be feasible in your own garden site. Style is, after all, a personal statement. What the styles do show, however, is that creating a garden with a distinct theme enhances the impact of the garden itself.

The Woodland Garden

Woodland on your property, even the tiniest grove, places you among the most fortunate of gardeners. If there is no woodland but you are willing to invest some effort and time in creating the effect, you can still enjoy the style of shade garden that for many people is the most magical and the easiest to maintain. But before you roll up your sleeves, first consider exactly what a woodland

garden is and how the style came about, then go about planning and establishing your woodland garden.

This style of shade gardening evolved in the late 19th century with the influential horticulturists William Robinson and Gertrude Jekyll, who favored "wild" or "natural" gardens over the traditional formal gardens composed of tender annuals. The new style was adaptable to the modest home or to the estate. It was a refreshing change from what Gertrude Jekyll termed the "parade of conscious effort" that characterized the Victorian style. A typical Robinson or Jekyll garden might have some relatively formal elements nearest the house and, in its farthest reaches, naturalistic woodland.

From *Gardens for Small Country Houses,* by Ger-

Top left: A formal garden relies heavily on symmetry and the geometric division of space. Bottom left: This shade garden in Larchmont, New York is a collector's garden, containing junipers, a prostrate form of hemlock, ferns, holly, and rhododendrons and azaleas. This is a spring-blooming garden; in summer, green predominates. Right: This naturalistic garden features native stone and an abundant planting of azaleas, ferns, baby's-tears, and aspidistra.

trude Jekyll and Lawrence Weaver, here is part of a description of a woodland garden she designed. It hints at the scope and subtlety of her concerns as a gardener.

Nearest the lawn are groups of rhododendron, very carefully chosen for colour, with hardy ferns and one of the smaller andromedas [*Pieris* species] filling up nearest the grass on the shade side. . . .

Of the lesser grassy ways into the wooded ground, one that passes under the shade of oaks and birches has groups of some of the beautiful wild ferns—male fern [*Dryopteris filix-mas*], lady fern [*Anthyrium filix-femina*], and dilated shield fern [*Dryopteris dilitata*] in the natural setting of mossy ground and whortle-berry [*Vaccinium corymbusum*] and a complete backing of bracken [*Pteridium aquilinium*], with here and there a flowery incident—a patch of trillium [*Trillium* species], and further back a . . . bold back grouping of Solomon's seal [*Polygonatum* species]. . . . The intention of all the paths . . . is to lead by an imperceptible gradation from one to the other [from relatively formal garden to woodland garden] by the simplest means that may be devised, showing on the way the beauty of some one or two good kinds of plants and placing them so that they look happy and at home.

One of the special properties of woodland is the long dormancy of most deciduous trees in its high canopy. This period of leaflessness allows late winter and early spring bloomers to flourish in the weak sun of the early season, then lie protected or dormant through the shady hot months. The edge of a woodland, perhaps in grass unclipped except when bulb foliage is dormant, is a perfect place for naturalizing bulbs. Robinson and Jekyll planted them in "drifts" or "cloud patterns"—dense masses that meander in an apparently natural fashion. In *The Wild Garden* Robinson wrote:

If in a spot where a wide carpet of grass spreads out in the sheltered bay of a plantation [a woodland], there be dotted the blue Appenine Anemone [*Anemone apennina*], any Snowdrops [*Galanthus* species], the Snowflake [*Leucojum* species], Crocuses in variety, Scilla, Grape Hyacinths [*Muscari* species], many Narcissi, the Wood Anemone [*Anemone nemorosa*], and any other Spring flowers liking the [acid] soil, we should have a picture of vernal beauty, the flowers relieved by grass, and the whole devoid of man's weakness for tracing wallpaper patterns where everything should be varied and changeful.

Using any of these bulbs mentioned above, or substituting others such as roman hyacinths, chionodoxas, trollius, alliums, erythroniums, frittilarias, or *Tulipa* species, you can create a similar effect in your garden. See the list on page 59, and see Ortho's book *All About Bulbs*. For "other spring flowers" that naturalize easily and beautifully, read about: *Aquilegia, Convallaria, Dicentra, Polygonatum, Thalictrum,* and *Viola odorata* in the *Plant Selection Guide*.

Consider this list of possibilities for other low, her-

Left: This patio area was placed to take advantage of the natural woodland features already existing on the lot to create an all-green retreat in the forest, highlighted with white furniture. Below: This formalized treatment of the woodland theme features a select plant list and mass plantings, proving once again that you don't need a great diversity of plant material to create a big impact. Kurume azaleas, boxwood, and flowering dogwood create a spring-time sight few can forget.

baceous plants for your woodland garden. When you read about them, note their particular seasons, their sizes and textures, and the colors of their flowers. Some serve as ground covers, others as clumps or specimens: *Agapanthus, Begonia × semperflorens,* and *Liriope.*

Of course, a woodland garden includes more than the canopy forming its roof and the bulbs and herbaceous plants carpeting its floor. For beauty and for variety of size, there should be shrubs and small trees, placed informally so that they do not heavily shade smaller plants or hide them from view. *Rhododendron* and *Pieris* have already been mentioned. Consider also these shrubs, both deciduous and evergreen: *Abelia, Aucuba, Buxus, Gaultheria, Hydrangea, Kalmia, Leucothoe, Mahonia, Pittosporum,* and *Vaccinium.*

Consider these small trees as long-term residents of the woodland, or as temporary residents to make shade until the canopy develops, if you are creating a woodland: *Acer palmatum, Cornus florida, Hamamelis,* and *Ligustrum.*

The photograph on this page (right) shows a distinctive woodland garden style that has developed in the Southeast, where plants of several heights are combined with spectacular results. The canopy is tall deciduous trees or pines that cast dappled shade. A typical understory is dogwood *(Cornus florida),* with an occasional holly *(Ilex opaca)* or a deciduous magnolia. Azaleas and camellias are the seasonally showy shrubs. Ground covers such as *Ajuga, Bergenia, Convallaria, Duchesnia, Epimedium, Mentha requienii, Pratia, Sagina,* and *Soleirolia,* as well as bulbs and ferns, carpet the woodland floor.

The shaded bog garden is a specialized woodland garden with a style all its own. A wet spot in your shade

garden can be an asset. Here is your chance to use such bold-textured plants as *Asarum, Caltha, Hosta, Polygonatum,* and *Trillium,* as well as water-loving ferns *Adiantum* and *Osmunda.* Other especially beautiful bog plants for shade are *Clethra, Iris kaempferi,* and *Mimulus.*

The following plants like moisture but need some drainage, so they can be situated at the edge of the bog: *Hemerocallis, Hosta,* and *Vaccinium.*

If your garden lacks a boggy spot, you can contrive a permanent seep to create one. Of course a tiny pool or a short stream, perhaps with one or two large rocks and a recirculating pump, can create a focal point of great beauty with very little water. After all, water—even as a small feature—is "the soul of garden," as Jekyll wrote. Just be sure to put some tiny mosquito fish into the water to keep the atmosphere from deteriorating.

The most disheartening obstacle that you might encounter in making a garden in an existing woodland is impenetrable mats of tree roots. Thinning roots, removing the weakest and some of the most crowded, can help, and pruning can increase needed light (see

pages 43 to 45). But after trying whatever plants you most desire, you may have to limit your efforts to some of those that compete successfully with tree roots—for example, *Agapanthus, Ajuga, Bergenia, Convallaria, Hedera, Soleirolia,* and *Vinca.*

If you are creating a woodland, choose trees that form a high canopy and send down deep roots. See Ortho's *The World of Trees,* or a local nursery expert.

Plants that get only surface water will develop surface roots, so if rain is infrequent or fails to penetrate far, start out your new trees—and maintain them—by using a hose-attached deep-watering spike. Or irrigate slowly over long periods, then dig down—carefully—to see how far the water has penetrated. A core sampler does least harm to roots.

A well-established woodland will have a deep layer of humus that conserves moisture, admits enough air to roots, and provides a medium for the roots of many herbaceous woodland plants. The constant decomposition of this humus will acidify the soil and provide nutrients for the plants. Only occasionally, under certain trees and with constant moisture, will woodland soil become too acidic for some woodland plants and require balancing with ground limestone or agricultural lime. More often, garden soil requires more acidity, achieved by adding quantities of organic materials to the soil, and perhaps some nitrogen to replace nitrogen consumed by bacteria that break down the organic materials.

A final consideration, before you draw up your plan and implement it: How much water are you willing—or able, under occasional drought conditions—to give your woodland garden? If you live in an area of regular summer rainfall, you need not worry about this prob-lem. But if you live in a summer-dry area, you must make a decision (and not just about a woodland garden). If you want the garden to maintain itself once established, or require only a very occasional deep watering, choose drought-tolerant plants and mulch them heavily. (See the list of Plants for Dry Spots on page 56, and read about them in the *Plant Selection Guide.*) Consider which plants are native to your area and other summer-dry areas. County agents, nursery experts, and staff members of nearby botanic gardens can be helpful.

If you develop a woodland garden and your particular project proves demanding in the early stages, take heart. A correspondent with William Robinson reported this about his woodland dell, five years in the making: "Visitors often say that the dell beats all the rest of the garden for beauty, and it certainly gives less trouble in the attainment."

The Oriental Garden

Gardens in the oriental style are to many people the subtlest and most beautiful. Because of its simplicity and informality, this style lends itself to nearly every garden space, including the shadiest. (In fact, shade has traditionally been part of the style.) The thoughtful selection and arrangement of just a few simple materials can transform your large shaded area or tiny nook into a special place for serenity and contemplation.

If you walk into an oriental garden in the United States, you might automatically think of it as Japanese. It might be—or it might be Chinese. The overwhelming likelihood, of course, is that the garden would be American, with an oriental flavor. A true Chinese garden has precise, traditional combinations of rocks, water, and plants. A true Japanese garden has these combinations too, but

also an intricacy of arrangement and symbolism that is obscure to most westerners.

The Chinese character representing *garden* is composed of two words: *land* and *water.* Interpret "land" to include plants, rocks, and mountains, "water" to include streams and lakes, and you have the basics of the traditional Chinese garden. The old Taoist concept of a garden was a country retreat among trees in the mountains, with streams and waterfalls. If a garden had to be in town, it should mirror nature. Still, it should have within its walls a stream (if only a dry stream bed of rocks, gravel, and sand); flowers; a carefully planned curving path creating illusions of space and distance and leading to new perspectives; and a mound giving the illusion of a mountain. The illusion could be further refined through the use of rocks on the mound. Rocks themselves came to be used as miniature mountains.

Every Chinese garden, large or small, was intimate. It was laid out so that it showed itself little by little rather than all at once. Pavilion doors and vantage points along the path framed particularly fine views and focused attention on beautiful details. Bending forward to draw water from a drinking basin might suddenly reveal an otherwise hidden wonder, perhaps a splendid rock or a peephole-view to a mountain peak.

The influence of Chinese garden design eventually spread to Korea, then on to Japan, where it was made peculiarly Japanese. The two main types of Japanese styles are "level gardens" and "gardens of artificial mountains." The "dry" garden is only one form of the first. A more recent development, historically, is the tea garden. It is far less austere than the flat garden, but nevertheless restrained. There are evergreen trees but few flowering plants. The flowers might serve only to mark the seasons. The evergreen trees are often pruned to accentuate their individual characters. The function of the tea garden is to serve as a path to and away from the teahouse. Invariably there are a stone lantern, a stone basin, and a well. The whole experience of moving through the garden is an exercise in detachment and meditation.

To lovers of gardens and nature, to whom the layers of elaborate symbolism and subtle meanings are per-

Top: This garden in the Japanese style is centered around a large pond and severely pruned trees and shrubs. The Japanese maple has been pruned to grow skyward, admitting light and allowing a more complete view of the garden. Above: A classic stone lantern with a planting of artillery fern and camellias. Right: In dense shade, the use of gravel can be a real problem solver. Planting includes Japanese maple, mahonia, liriope, and aucuba.

haps inaccessible, Japanese and Chinese gardens can still be beautiful. Much that is Far Eastern can be adapted to an American garden.

Maybe you have only a dark, rather dank spot where you want a simple garden. If you are fortunate and live in an area where moss forms on the north side of trees and rocks, you might make a garden with a stone lantern (or a concrete facsimile), white river rocks, which will brighten the area and gather moss, a few larger rocks, and a few ferns that thrive in deep shade, such as *Adiantum* and *Polystichum*.

Various dwarf ornamental conifers are naturals for a lightly shaded Far Eastern garden. You might work *Chamaecyparis* species and *Cryptomeria* species into whatever plan you develop.

Azaleas and camellias are oriental. In traditional Japanese gardens azaleas are used very sparingly for color—in fact, they are often kept sheared and compact, so that there are few if any blossoms, although a fully blossoming plant or cluster of plants may be used as an accent. As long as you don't use too many colors, you can use azaleas as part of your design without destroying the traditional oriental feeling. You can use camellias too, for larger, bolder-textured effects, although you risk getting away from traditional style here. Remember that both plants like deep, well-drained acid soil, and that they should never be allowed to dry out. *Camellia sasanqua* makes an especially effective espalier, although *C. japonica* and *C. reticulata* can also be used.

If you want trees to create shade, consider pines, flowering plums, cherries, crabapples, beeches, the larger Japanese maples, ginkgo, and *Magnolia soulangiana*.

Among the many plants suited to shaded areas of oriental gardens are *Buxus, Liriope,* and *Ophiopogon*.

Whatever combinations you choose, remember oriental restraint and understatement. A Japanese maple, a few small evergreens, some tufts of dwarf bamboo, one flowering plant, pebbles, a flat, weathered bench, and a lantern might fill a large space adequately and beautifully. A tiny pool (perhaps a birdbath top) sunken among rocks and ferns, and a beautifully shaped, subtly pruned dwarf *Pieris* might create a world inside a tiny shaded courtyard.

Shade garden specialties

The following lists of shade-tolerant plants are designed to help you select plants to fill special needs in your garden. Is your garden dry and very shady? Lightly shaded and moist? Are you looking for a bright-flowering annual to grow in medium shade? Consult these lists, then read about those plants that interest you in the *Plant Selection Guide,* beginning on page 61. Use the lists to spark your imagination or to solve landscaping problems. Keep in mind that, in many cases, when a name appears on a list, only selected varieties (usually too numerous to mention in the list) may fit the given category. Some of them may not flower or flower poorly in the colder zones. Consult the *Plant Selection Guide,* seed catalogs, and local experts to help pinpoint the variety best suited to your needs.

Each plant on these lists is given a shade tolerance rating between 1 and 4. These numbers refer to degree of shade: 1 and 2 are types of light shade, 3 is medium shade, and 4 is dense shade. For complete definitions of these categories, see page 8.

Perennials for Shade	Flower Color	Shade Tolerance
Acanthus mollis	White	1–3
Agapanthus species	White, blue	1–3
Anemone species	White, pink, red, purple, blue	1,2
Aquilegia species and hybrids	All colors and combinations	1,2
Aruncus dioicus	Ivory white	1,2
Astilbe hybrids	White, pink, red	1–3
Brunnera macrophylla	Sky blue	1,2
Caltha palustris	Yellow	1,2
Chrysogonum virginianum	Yellow	1,2
Cimicifuga racemosa	White	1
Clivia miniata	Orange	1–4
Dicentra species	Rose pink	1–3
Digitalis species and hybrids	Yellow, buff, purple, white, pink	1–4
Doronicum cordatum	Yellow	1,2
Echinacea purpurea	Purple	1,2
Helleborus niger	White	1,2
Hemerocallis species and hybrids	Yellow, orange, red, pink	1,2
Hosta species	Blue, white	1–4
Iris kaempferi	Blue, violet, white	1,2
Ligularia dentata	Yellow	1,2
Liriope species	Blue, white	1–3
Lobelia cardinalis	Crimson	1,2
Mertensia virginica	Violet/blue	1–4
Ophiopogon japonicus	Blue	1–3
Polygonatum species	White	1–4
Primula species	All colors, some bicolor	1–3
Pulmonaria saccharata	Blue, silver-spotted foliage	1–4
Rehmannia elata	Rose-violet, spotted	1,2
Tradescantia virginiana	White, pink, magenta, purple, blue	1–4
Trillium species	White, pink, maroon	1–3
Trollius europaeus	Yellow	1–3

Plants for Deep Shade	Foliage/Flower Color	Type of Plant
Asarum species	Deep green/brown	Ground cover
Aucuba japonica	Variegated/red berries	Shrub
Bergenia cordifolia	Light green/pink	Ground cover
Browallia speciosa	Deep green/blue, white	Annual
Clivia miniata	Med. green/orange	Perennial
Digitalis purpurea and hybrids	Med. green/yellow, buff, purple, white, pink	Perennial
Dryopteris	Med. green	Fern
Epimedium species	Med. green/white, pink, yellow	Ground cover
Fatsia japonica	Tropical appearance	Shrub
Gaultheria procumbens	Deep green/white; red berries	Ground cover
Hedera species	Lt.–deep green, yellow, white	Ground cover
Hosta species	Deep green/blue, white	Perennial
Hydrangea macrophylla	Lt. green/white, pink, red, violet, blue	Shrub
Impatiens wallerana	Med. green/mauve, pink, orange, white, red, rose, salmon	Annual
Kerria japonica	Lt. green/yellow	Shrub
Leucothoe fontanesiana	Bronze new growth, variegated	Shrub
Mertensia virginica	Deep green/violet, blue	Perennial
Mimulus species	Deep green/yellow, maroon	Annual
Pachysandra terminalis	Lt.–med. green/white	Ground cover
Pittosporum tobira	Dark green/white/	Shrub
Polygonatum species	Med. green/white	Perennial
Polystichum species	Med. green	Fern
Pulmonaria saccharata	Deep green/all colors, bicolor	Perennial
Sarcococca ruscifolia	Med. green/white/blue berries	Shrub
Soleirolia soleirolii	Lt. green	Ground cover
Taxus species	Deep blue-green needles/red berries	Shrub
Torenia fournieri	Med. green/blue, yellow, violet	Annual
Tradescantia virginiana	Deep green/white, pink, blue, magenta, purple	Perennial

Dicentra eximia, Polystichum acrostichoides

Polygonatum odoratum

Plants for Dry Spots	Type	Shade Tolerance
Acanthus mollis	Perennial	1–3
Aucuba japonica	Shrub	1–4
Bergenia cordifolia	Ground cover	1–4
Cercis canadensis	Tree	1,2
Cornus canadensis	Ground cover	1,2
Duchesnea indica	Ground cover	1–3
Euonymus fortunei	Shrub or ground cover	1–3
Festuca ovina glauca	Grass	1,2
Hemerocallis species and hybrids	Herbaceous perennial	1,2
Kerria japonica	Shrub or vine	1–4
Ligustrum species	Shrub or tree	1–3
Mahonia species	Shrub or ground cover	1–3
Nierembergia hippomanica	Annual	1,2
Polygonatum commutatum	Perennial	1–4
Pratia angulata	Ground cover	1–3
Sarcococca ruscifolia	Shrub	1–4
Tradescantia virginiana	Perennial	1–4
Vinca minor, vinca major	Ground cover	1–3

Plants for Wet Spots	Type	Shade Tolerance
Aesculus species	Shrub or tree	1–3
Aruncus dioicus	Perennial	1,2
Asarum species	Ground cover	1–4
Astilbe species and hybrids	Perennial	1–3
Caltha palustris	Perennial	1,2
Calycanthus species	Shrub	1,2
Clethra alnifolia	Shrub	1,2
Convallaria majalis	Perennial	1–3
Doronicum cordatum	Perennial	1,2
Hemerocallis species and hybrids	Perennial	1,2
Hosta species	Perennial	1–4
Ilex species	Shrub or tree	1–3
Iris kaempferi	Perennial	1,2
Ligularia dentata	Perennial	1,2
Lobelia cardinalis	Perennial	1,2
Mahonia species	Shrub	1–3
Mertensia virginica	Perennial	1–4
Mimulus species and hybrids	Annual	1–4
Myosotis sylvatica	Annual	1–3
Pulmonaria saccharata	Perennial	1–4
Soleirolia soleirolii	Ground cover	1–4
Tradescantia virginiana	Perennial	1–4

Caltha palustris

Euonymus fortunei

Ground Covers for Shade	Foliage/Flower Color	Shade Tolerance
Ajuga reptans	Variegated, green, bronze/blue	1–3
Asarum caudatum	Deep green/brown	1–4
Bergenia cordifolia	Light green/pink	1–4
Convallaria majalis	Deep green/white	1–3
Cornus canadensis	Deep green/white/red berries	1,2
Duchesnea indica	Med. green/yellow/red berries	1–3
Epimedium species	Med. green/white, pink, yellow	1–4
Euonymus fortunei	Deep green, variegated	1–3
Festuca ovina glauca	Silvery blue	1,2
Fragaria chiloensis	Deep green/white	1,2
Gaultheria procumbens	Deep green/white/red berries	1–4
Hakonechloa macra	Variegated creamy white	1,2
Hedera species	Deep–lt. green, yellow, white	1–4
Hosta species	All shades, variegated/white, blue	1–4
Liriope species	Yellow or white variegation/blue, white	1–3
Mahonia repens	Deep green, bronze/yellow	1–3
Mentha requienii	Light green/pink	1,2
Ophiopogon japonicus	Deep green/blue	1–3
Pachysandra terminalis	Med.–lt. green/white	1–4
Pratia angulata	Med. green/white/violet berries	1–3
Sagina subulata	Lt. or dark green/white	1,2
Soleirolia soleirolii	Lt. green	1–4
Vancouveria hexandra	Med. green/white	1–3
Vinca minor, vinca major	Deep green/blue	1–3

Annual Color for Shade	Flower Color	Shade Tolerance
Begonia × semperflorens-cultorum	White, pink, rose, red	1–3
Browallia speciosa	Blue, white	1–4
Campanula medium	Blue, pink, white	1,2
Clarkia species (Godetias)	Pink, salmon, red, white	1,2
Coleus hybrids	Blue; foliage red, purple, yellow	1–3
Impatiens balsamina	Red, pink, white	1
Impatiens wallerana	Mauve, pink, orange, white, rose, salmon, red, magenta	1–4
Mimulus species	Yellow, maroon	1–4
Myosotis sylvatica	Sky blue	1–3
Nicotiana alata	White, lime, pink, deep rose	1–3
Nierembergia hippomanica	Blue	1,2
Salvia splendens	Red, white	1,2
Torenia fournieri	Blue, violet, yellow	1–4
Viola hybrids	All colors	1–3

Understory Trees	Flower Color	Shade Tolerance
Acer palmatum	Green	1,2
Aesculus species	White, deep rose	1–3
Cercis species	Pink	1,2
Cornus florida	White, pink	1
Hamamelis × intermedia	Yellow	1,2
Ligustrum species	White	1–3
Tsuga canadensis	Brown cones	1

Acer palmatum

Ferns, hosta, iris, ligularia, petisites, rhododendron

Flowering Shrubs for Shade	Color	Shade Tolerance
Abelia × grandiflora	Lavender/white	1–3
Aesculus parviflora	White	1–3
Aesculus pavia	Red (deep rose)	1–3
Camellia japonica	White, pink, red	1–3
Camellia sasanqua	White, pink, red	1,2
Clethra alnifolia	White	1,2
Fuchsia species and hybrids	Red, pink, white, blue, purple	1–3
Hydrangea macrophylla	White, pink, red, violet, blue	1–4
Kalmia latifolia	Pink, white	1,2
Kerria japonica	Yellow	1–4
Mahonia species	Yellow; blue berries	1–3
Pieris japonica	White, pink; red new growth	1–3
Rhododendron species and hybrids	All colors	1–3
Sarcococca ruscifolia	White, blue berries	1–4

58

Foliage Shrubs for Shade	Height/Point of Interest	Shade Tolerance
Aucuba japonica	To 6'/brilliant variegation/red berries	1–4
Buxus sempervirens	To 10'/excellent for formal training	1–3
Calycanthus floridus	To 10'/fragrant maroon flowers	1,2
Chamaecyparis species	To 5'/most elegant in habit	1,2
Euonymus fortunei	To 2'/some with variegated foliage	1–3
Fatsia japonica	To 15'/tropical appearance	1–4
Gaultheria shallon	To 5'/red berries, white flowers	1–4
Ilex species	To 20'/red berries	1–3
Leucothoe fontanesiana	To 5'/bronze new growth; variegated	1–4
Ligustrum species	To 25'/white flowers if unpruned	1–3
Nandina domestica	To 8'/red-bronze foliage	1–3
Osmanthus species	To 10'/insignificant but fragrant flowers	1–3
Pittosporum tobira	To 10'/white flowers, orange berries	1–4
Taxus species	To 50'/deep blue-green needles, red berries	1–4
Vaccinium ovatum	To 12'/small white flowers, blue berries	1–3

Most bulbs need bright sunlight, but a few enjoy shade. Spring bulbs that like bright sun, such as daffodils, do well underneath deciduous trees with high branches. These trees allow light to reach the bulb during the critical spring months. Bulbs that do particularly well in the shade include the following.

Bulbs and Bulblike Plants for Shade	Color	Shade Tolerance
Begonia × *tuberhybrida*	White, yellow, bronze, pink, orange	1–3
Caladium hybrids	Foliage red, pink, white	1–3
Convallaria majalis	White, pink	1–3
Cyclamen species	White, pink	1,2
Erythronium species	Yellow, pink, white	1–3
Fritillaria meleagris	Cream, maroon	1,2
Leucojum species	White	1
Scilla	Blue, purple, pink, white	1,2

Leucojum aestivum

Aucuba japonica 'Sulphurea'

PLANT SELECTION GUIDE

Use this list of over one hundred shade-loving annual and perennial flowers, shrubs, trees, and ground covers, together with the information in Chapter 4, to help you plan and design your shade garden, and to determine the needs of the plants you already have.

Gardening in the shade can be a challenge for the experienced as well as for the novice gardener. The most critical aspect is selecting an appropriate plant for the shade situation in your garden. The selection of shade-loving plants is endless, including evergreen and deciduous shrubs, ground covers, bulbs, and annual and perennial flowers. This selection guide presents the wide diversity of plants available. For each plant we have included its shade tolerance, zones of adaptation (particularly important in areas with cold winters), cultural requirements, and special features such as fragrance and blossom color that make the plant particularly desirable.

Read through this selection guide, noting the plants that catch your eye. Or check the handy shade plant selection lists on pages 55 to 59 to guide you quickly to the best choice for specific garden situations such as acid or alkaline soil or drought. Then, for a complete description of the plant and its needs, return to this selection guide.

The plants are listed alphabetically by *genus*, the broad grouping into which plants with similar botanical characteristics are categorized. If a particular *species* within the genus is recommended, then that species name follows. Otherwise, if all species in the genus are recommended, then just the word "species" is listed. A subgrouping within a particular species is the *cultivar,* or horticultural variety. A cultivar is very similar to other members of the species, but a minor characteristic such as leaf color or size sets it apart from the other members of the species, and it is given a separate name. The cultivar's name is denoted by single quotation marks. To make this nomenclature more clear, follow this example: *Buxus microphylla* 'Wintergreen'; *Buxus* is the genus, *microphylla* is the species, and 'Wintergreen' is the cultivar. The common names given are those most commonly accepted in the gardening world. If you are accustomed to gardening in the sun, some of the plants listed will be new to you; and some may be old favorites that you didn't know were also tolerant of the shade.

Left: This entrance area with open shade is a good environment for a variety of colorful plants: impatiens, variegated coleus, a standard fuchsia next to the door, and climbing hydrangeas against the stone wall. Right: Evergreen shrubs, rhododendrons and azaleas of medium height, and evergreen and deciduous trees of various sizes fill in all levels of this pleasing landscape.

Abelia × grandiflora

Acanthus mollis

ABELIA × GRANDIFLORA

Glossy Abelia
Broad-leafed deciduous to
evergreen shrub
Medium shade to full sun
Hardy to Zone 6

The hardiest and most free-
flowering of the abelias, this hybrid makes an effective specimen,
informal hedge, or mass planting,
combining particularly well with
broad-leafed evergreens. Showy,
pinkish white flowers cover the
plant from July until frost. The
fine-textured, glossy, deep green
summer foliage turns an attractive
bronze in the fall. It is deciduous
to semievergreen in the North
and increasingly evergreen the
farther south it is grown. The
habit is graceful, rounded, and
arching. It grows at a medium to
fast rate, reaching 4 to 8 feet
high and wide.

Give glossy abelia well-drained
soil, medium shade to full sun,
and average watering, and it will
prove to be an easy-to-grow, pest-
free plant. In dense shade, the
habit is leggy and flowering is
sparse. Expect frequent winter
dieback in northern Zone 6,
although the new growth will
come back quickly. Older, overgrown shrubs can be renewed by
cutting back hard, almost to the
ground, in late winter or early
spring.

While glossy abelia can be
sheared easily into formal shapes,
doing so seriously reduces flowering. It is probably best to allow
it to achieve its graceful, natural
shape.

Lower forms, such as 'Prostrata'
and 'Sherwoodii', make excellent
large-scale ground covers and
bank covers.

ACANTHUS MOLLIS

Bear's Breech, Acanthus
Perennial
Medium shade to full sun
Hardy to Zone 8

Bear's breech is grown for its
clumps of immense, coarse, glossy
leaves and tall flower spikes. It is
usually considered more a landscape plant than a border
perennial.

The dark green, deeply lobed
leaves grow to 2 feet long, in
basal clusters often 2 feet high
and 4 feet wide. The foliage is imposing and effective from March
to October. The flowers are
creamy white, lavender, or rose,
with greenish or purplish bracts,
and appear along upright stems
2 to 3 feet tall. They bloom in late
spring and early summer.

Bear's breech does best in
moist, rich loam with good drainage, but it performs reasonably
well in dry sandy soil. It prefers
filtered shade, but tolerates full
sun in cool climates. It tolerates
drought, but the foliage will be
more lush with adequate moisture. In the northern limits of its
range, plant in a warm, protected
location, and mulch over winter.
Space plants 3 to 4 feet apart.

Care is easy. Remove spent
flower stalks. To grow for foliage
alone, remove stalks as they appear. Bear's breech is a very invasive plant. The roots spread a
considerable distance underground and the plant forms
spreading clumps, like bamboo,
so confine the roots unless you
want a large stand. Snails and
slugs can be a problem. The plant
rarely requires division for rejuvenation, but is easily propagated
by that method. Divide any time
from October to March.

ACER PALMATUM

Japanese Maple
Deciduous tree
Light shade to full sun
Hardy to Zone 5

Japanese maple is the aristocrat of
small trees for light shade. All
forms are deciduous, but in size,
habit, color, and texture there
is enormous variation. Even in old
age, the smallest Japanese maples
remain low mounds or miniatures
of great character and grace. The
taller forms become small trees,
no taller than 20 feet. A grafted
specimen of a given variety generally remains smaller than a seedling specimen.

Flowers are small, delicate, and
inconspicuous, appearing in spring
before the tree is in leaf. The
pendulous clusters of winged
seeds are showier.

Some varieties, if given enough
light, have foliage that is deep
red until autumn, when the color
changes; some have red foliage
only in spring; others have bright
green, deep green, bronze-tinged,
or variegated foliage. Some have
simply-lobed leaves, others have
leaves cut as elaborately as lacy
snowflakes.

The taller forms are useful for
creating an understory beneath a
high, thin tree canopy or for
planting on the north or east sides
of buildings. Smaller types, the
dwarfs, make dramatic accents in
oriental settings, in planters
(sometimes as bonsai), and in
various focal points. Choose a site
sheltered from hot, drying summer winds; cold, drying winter
winds; and late frosts—all of
which burn and curl leaf tips. The
laceleaf types are most vulnerable. Well-drained, acid soil, moist
and rich in organic matter, is
important.

In the coldest zones, the roots
of container plants need extra
protection in winter. Use heavy
mulch, insulate around the container, or sink the container into
the ground. Water frequently
in hot weather.

There are hundreds of varieties
of Japanese maples. 'Aconitifol-
ium', a dwarf, has deeply cut
green leaves.

'Atropurpureum' is especially
hardy and is similar to the species
in its relatively uncut leaves and
its size (up to 20 feet but usually
smaller). Leaves are purple or
purple-bronze.

'Bloodgood', quite similar to
'Atropurpureum', is the deepest
red of all the Japanese maples.

'Burgundy Lace' is smaller and
its leaves are far more deeply
cut than those of 'Atropurpureum'. It is very hardy.

Acer palmatum

Adiantum pedatum

Agapanthus africanus

A.p. var. *dissectum* (Laceleaf or Threadleaf Maple) is a gracefully spreading, weeping dwarf with very finely cut leaves. It seldom reaches 8 feet in height. There are many forms. 'Crimson Queen' has especially deep red leaves. 'Flavescens' has bright yellowish green leaves. 'Ever Red' is purplish red and mounding. 'Garnet' is similar but slightly more vigorous. 'Ornatum' is bright red and has especially bright autumn foliage; it is very hardy. 'Oshio Beni' ('Oshu beni') is very like 'Atropurpureum' but has longer branches. 'Roseo-marginata', 'Tricolor', and 'Versicolor' have variegated foliage, respectively pink-edged, spotted with red, pink, and white, and variegated white, pink, and light green. 'Butterfly' has cream-colored variegations against bluish to pale green.

'Sango Kaku' ('Senkaki'), a bright-green-leafed variety, makes a spectacular winter display of coral-red branches. It grows upright to around 10 feet, taller when grown from a seedling.

A. circinatum (Vine Maple), a deciduous shrub or a small multistemmed tree native to the West Coast, is similar to *A. palmatum* and has similar uses in the garden. Like the other species it grows best in some shade except in gentlest climates. It is also rather small, 6 to 8 feet as a shrub, 20 feet or higher as a tree. It likes rich soil and moisture, and will tolerate wetness. In a moist, sheltered spot with medium shade, it may sprawl and vine a bit. This form can be particularly attractive against a shaded wall or as an understory tree in a woodland garden.

ADIANTUM PEDATUM

Maidenhair Fern
Fern
Medium shade to medium sun
Hardy to Zone 4

Adiantum pedatum is a hardy maidenhair fern native throughout most of North America. Fronds are delicate in appearance but are wiry, growing to 2 feet high. The plant spreads by creeping root stalks, making a beautiful, fine-textured ground cover. Moist, cool soil with a leaf mold mulch is necessary to keep the delicate fibrous roots from drying out. Medium shade is best, although considerable sun is tolerated. This fern will naturalize well with wild flowers in a native garden. It also thrives in the shade of taller-growing rhododendrons and similar shrubs, or tucked into the pockets of a stone wall.

AESCULUS PARVIFLORA

Bottlebrush Buckeye
Deciduous shrub
Medium shade to full sun
Zones 5 to 8

Spectacular late-season flowers, trouble-free foliage (unusual for the buckeyes), and adaptability to heavy shade make this shrub an excellent subject for a specimen, or for massing and clumping in problem shady areas, such as under large shade trees. Not a shrub for small areas, its open, wide-spreading (8 to 15 feet), suckering habit can be troublesome if not given enough room to grow. The flowers are profuse, large, erect clusters that grow 8 to 12 inches long, are white with red anthers, and bloom from early to late July.

Bottlebrush buckeye prefers moist, well-drained soil that is high in organic matter, and it tolerates medium shade to full sun.

'Roger's' is a superior cultivar that is worth seeking out. It produces huge flower clusters, 18 to 30 inches long, two weeks later than the species, and does not exhibit the suckering habit.

Aesculus pavia (Red Buckeye; Zones 6 to 8), like bottlebrush buckeye, is relatively resistant to most of the leaf diseases that plague the buckeyes. Mildew can be a problem. However, it will not affect this shrub's long-term vigor. Red buckeye differs from bottlebrush buckeye by having bright red flowers in early spring. It is also less hardy. In size and form it is much the same. *A. pavia* 'Atrosanguinea' has darker red flowers, while 'Humilis' is a low, often prostrate form.

AGAPANTHUS

Lily-of-the-Nile
Perennial
Medium shade to full sun
Hardy to Zone 8

Agapanthus is a summer-flowering perennial native to South Africa. It does best in good garden soil but accepts heavy soil. Medium shade is tolerated, although it will flower more in light shade to full sun. Ample water is recommended, particularly when the plant is in flower. Flower stalks should be removed after bloom. Divide clumps every five or six years. Agapanthus is easy to grow in mild-winter climates (it is hardy to 15°F), and is seldom bothered by pests. There are both evergreen and deciduous varieties, but all have leathery, strap-like leaves and fleshy roots, varying in size and flower color.

A. orientalis is most commonly cultivated. Its leaves are evergreen, about 2 feet long and 2 inches wide. Flower stalks (to 4 or 5 feet) bear many separate flowers; white, double blue, and giant blue varieties are available. This giant species is often mistakenly sold as *A. africanus* or *A. umbellatus*.

A. africanus is a smaller version of *A. orientalis*. Leaves are narrow (½ inch), and flower stalks reach to 1½ feet.

A. inapertus is deciduous, with dark blue flowers that hang from 4 to 5-foot flower stalks. Leaves are 2 inches wide and 2½ feet long.

'Dwarf White' agapanthus is evergreen, 1½ feet tall, and bears white flowers on 2-foot stalks.

'Peter Pan' is also evergreen and very dwarf, 8 to 12 inches tall. Blue flowers are clustered on top of 15-inch stalks.

Anemone × hybrida

Ajuga reptans

Aquilegia

Ajuga, Carpet Bugle, Bugleweed
Ground cover
Medium to light shade
Hardy to Zone 6

Lushness, brief but showy flowering, and rapidly spreading, tight growth make ajuga one of the most useful ground covers for medium to light shade. This evergreen perennial is sometimes used as a grass substitute in small to medium-sized areas, especially on slopes. Because it is shallow rooted, it makes a satisfactory cover for small bulbs. It is also useful around shrubs, in shaded parking strips, in moist rock gardens, and in the front of mixed borders. Foliage of smaller varieties is about 2 inches tall; foliage of larger varieties is 3 or 4 inches tall.

From spring to early summer, bright blue or blue-purple flowers appear on spikes usually 4 to 6 inches above the foliage. Individual flowers are small, but the mass of spikes is striking.

Leaves are oval to roundish, 3 to 5 inches long, 2 to 4 inches wide, in tight, glossy rosettes. Bronze or variegated leaves of some varieties contrast interestingly with other foliage in the garden. Green ajugas redden at first frost.

Moist, rich soil and good drainage are necessary for healthy, long-lived ajuga. Inadequate drainage can lead to root rot. Ajuga needs air circulation and brightness—light shade, or medium to light shade in hotter, drier areas. Space plants 6 to 12 inches apart, a bit farther for the big varieties. Stepping stones aid in maintenance, as ajuga will tolerate little or no foot traffic.

Care is moderately easy. Brightness, air circulation, and good drainage minimize the likelihood of root rot, powdery mildew, and root-knot nematodes. Use appropriate sprays if necessary. Spikes may be clipped after flowering.

A. r. atropurpurea has brown foliage. So does 'Giant Bronze', whose leaves are larger and somewhat metallic. 'Giant Green', also large, has clear green leaves. 'Jungle Bronze' and 'Jungle Green' are both large, particularly the latter, with 8 to 10-inch spikes. *A. r. rubra* has dark, purplish foliage. The leaves of *A. r. variegata* are edged and dappled with creamy yellow. Other varieties are occasionally offered at nurseries.

Japanese Anemone
Perennial
Light shade to full sun
Hardy to Zone 6

The Japanese anemone displays attractive foliage and loose, open clusters of flowers in white and shades of pink. It is especially valuable for providing fall color in partial shade.

The flowers are each 1½ to 3 inches across, depending on variety and conditions of growth, and bloom in late summer to midautumn. The leaves are dark to light green, large, deeply lobed, and pleasantly coarse in texture. Reminiscent of maple leaves, they are quite effective, especially during the bloom period. They cover the plant densely at the bottom and become smaller and more scarce toward the top, leaving the upper 1 to 2 feet of stem bare. Japanese anemones grow 2 to 5 feet tall.

The plants increase slowly in size and number of flowering stems. They are well-behaved, long-lived in favorable locations, and resent disturbance once established. They need rich, moist soil that is high in humus. Soil must have excellent drainage; wet soil in winter is usually fatal. The plants prefer light shade but tolerate full sun, especially in cool climates. Space them 18 inches apart.

Care is moderately easy. Water during dry spells in summer. In the northern limits of their hardiness range it is advisable to protect plants with a loose mulch, such as evergreen boughs. Do not apply this protection until the ground is frozen, however, or trapped moisture will kill the plants. The black blister beetle can quickly defoliate established plants.

Clumps rarely require division. If necessary, divide in early spring. For increase, root cuttings are better.

Columbine
Perennial
Light shade to full sun
Hardy to Zone 3

Columbines are delicate, airy plants with curiously spurred, showy flowers in a wide range of colors and forms. They are useful in borders and in "wild" gardens. They prefer filtered, light shade, but will take full sun in moderate climates. These ideal woodland plants need cool, moist soil that is rich in organic matter.

The flowers, which appear in May and June, come in shades of white, blue, purple, red, pink, yellow, orange, reddish brown, and nearly black, in solids or bicolors. Each bloom consists of five sepals and five tubular petals that extend into spurs beyond the

Asarum europeaum

rear of the blossom. Hybridizers have developed a huge array not only of color but of flower size, from 1½ to 4 inches across and up to 6 inches long. The flowers nod gracefully at the ends of long, slender stems.

The foliage is light green, often with a slight silvery, dusty cast that catches and holds dewdrops. Notched compound leaves give the plant an open, finely textured appearance somewhat like that of maidenhair fern. Foliage can be effective into August, if not attacked by leaf miners. The plant grows from 18 to 36 inches tall.

Columbine is usually short-lived, especially if the soil does not have perfect drainage. It does self-sow in favorable environments, but the offspring will differ, often radically, from hybrid parents.

ARUNCUS DIOICUS

Goatsbeard
Perennial
Light shade to full sun
Hardy to Zone 4

Goatsbeard, formerly listed as *A. sylvester*, is a large, shrublike perennial that produces showy, silky white plumes in midsummer. The plant suggests a large astilbe, and is excellent in partial shade in the rear of the border or as a shrub accent, particularly in combination with astilbe.

The flowers are minute and gathered into the gracefully relaxed plumes, which are often as long as 16 inches. They appear in mid-June to early July. The foliage is medium green with large, compound leaves of bold texture. It is effective all season long. The plant grows 5 to 7 feet tall, spreading 3 to 5 feet across. It is long-lived and, despite its large size, restrained in growth and not invasive.

Aruncus needs moist, preferably rich soil that is high in organic matter. It grows best in light shade, such as under a high canopy of trees or on the east side of a building, but with sufficient moisture it tolerates full sun. Space plants 3 to 5 feet apart.

Care is easy. Water aruncus generously and deeply. Fertilize regularly during the growing season. Despite its height, it never needs staking. It has no serious pests, can go many years before needing division for rejuvenation. Division for increase is difficult and rarely successful.

ASARUM

Wild Ginger
Ground cover
Dense to light shade
Hardiness varies according to species

The wild gingers are incomparable ground covers for the heavily shaded, woodland soils to which they are native. They are especially attractive combined with evergreen shrubs or wildflowers in a naturalistic setting. Although not related to culinary ginger, the creeping rootstalks and pungent leaves have a gingerlike fragrance. They have 2 to 7-inch heart-shaped leaves on 7 to 10-inch stalks. Flowers are minute and appear in early spring.

The gingers are native to woodlands where the shade is heavy and the soil is high in humus and moisture. With lots of water they will grow in heavy soils, but do best in either native or generously amended soil. Locations protected from drying winds are best. Propagate by division of the creeping rootstalks.

There are several species, both deciduous and evergreen, with variations in leaf size and color.

Astilbe

A. caudatum (British Columbia Wild Ginger) is evergreen and probably the most commonly available species. *A. europeaum* (European Wild Ginger) is virtually identical to *A. caudatum* except for its more shiny, glossy leaves. Both are hardy to Zone 5. Other evergreens are *A. arifolium* and *A. virginicum*. They are similar except for reduced cold tolerance; they are hardy to Zone 6.

Deciduous types are native over much of the eastern United States. The dried creeping root of *A. canadense* (Canadian Wild Ginger) is used as a ginger substitute. It is one of the most hardy, to Zone 4.

A. shuttleworthii is similar but has thinner, mottled, usually larger leaves and is hardy only to Zone 7. The deciduous forms are not cultivated as frequently as the evergreen ones because of the lack of winter effect.

ASTILBE

False Spires; Astilbe
Perennial
Medium shade to full sun
Hardy to Zone 4

Astilbe is a favorite perennial for cool, moist locations with medium to light shade, and with deep, rich soil that is high in organic matter. It does not tolerate wet winters well without adequate drainage, and will not take summer drought. It performs well in deep shade but accepts full sun if watered deeply and often. Space plants 1 to 2 feet apart.

Astilbe offers glossy, dark green foliage and fluffy plumes of white, pink, lavender, or red flowers on erect or arching stems. The tiny flowers are produced in great quantities, and the effect is delicate and feathery. It blooms in June and July.

The leaves are divided and compound. Sometimes tinged with bronze, they resemble a fern and are always lush and refined. The foliage forms bushy mounds rarely exceeding 2 feet in height; the flowers often reach another 12 to 18 inches. Most flower heads are erect and pyramidal; others arch gracefully.

Astilbe will gradually spread as clumps expand. A heavy feeder, it will deplete the soil and flower less as the years go by; but division every 3 or 4 years will rejuvenate the flowering. The plant is restrained in growth, not invasive, and long-lived.

Aucuba japonica var. *variegata*

Begonia (fibrous-rooted)

Bergenia crassifolia

Japanese Aucuba
Evergreen shrub
Dense to light shade
Hardy to Zone 7

A female aucuba was introduced to England in 1783; but not until nearly a century later, after a male plant had been imported, were the English able to see aucuba's scarlet berries. Beautiful though the berries are, it is probably aucuba's bold, varied, evergreen foliage and its suitability for dense shade that have made it one of the most popular plants for shady gardens. Aucuba flourishes in spots so dark that little grows well, and the foliage of variegated forms adds brightness. If unpruned, it grows at a moderate rate to 6 to 10 feet high, but becomes leggy and open. Therefore, well-grown aucuba is usually seen as a shrub pruned to a dense, rounded form. It is often used as a large container plant.

The tiny mahogany flowers are very inconspicuous, but the ¾-inch berries are showy. The glossy, serrated leaves are 4 to 7 inches long, and 2 to 3 inches wide.

Aucuba will accept nearly any soil but grows best in rich, moist, well-drained soil. Tree roots are usually no problem for it.

Japanese aucuba is drought-tolerant once established, although it looks better in moist, well-drained soil with high organic content. Instead of shearing, prune it to leaf nodes in winter. It is susceptible to spider mites and mealybugs.

Some of the most popular, commonly available varieties are:

A. j. crassifolia is a male with thick green leaves.

A. j. dentata, female, has small, coarsely serrated green leaves.

A. j. longifolia is a free-fruiting female with long leaves.

A. j. nana is green-leafed, smaller than the species.

A. j. crotonifolia is a male with green leaves spotted white.

A. j. picturata is a female with a large yellow blotch in the center of a spotted green leaf.

A. j. variegata, available in both sexes, has gold-flecked green leaves. It is usually known as gold dust plant.

For information on *Azalea*, see *Color in the Shade*, pages 14–17.

Wax Begonia; Fibrous-rooted Begonia
Perennial used as an annual
Medium to light shade

Fibrous-rooted begonias are popular annuals that grow well in medium to light shade. They need rich, well-drained soil and plenty of fertilizer. Flowers appear in shades of pink, white, and red. Foliage is green, bronze, mahogany with a reddish tint, or variegated green and white. Most grow to 6 to 12 inches; a few varieties reach 16 inches.

Begonias call to mind the lavishness of Victorian estate gardening. Such gardening at the turn of the century was marked by a taste for the exotic and curious, by the ability to support hothouses, and by the new-found glory of scientific hybridization. All three seemed to be epitomized in the begonia, and the fibrous-rooted annuals of this genus quickly became one of the most important plants for bedding and edging, particularly in the shade.

Unlike many other annuals of that era, however, begonias have, if anything, increased in popularity. Blessed with a wide range of attributes, including an easy nature tolerant of abuse, adaptability to medium or light shade, a compact floriferous habit, wide variety in form and flower shape, long-season effectiveness, and the dual attraction of both colorful foliage and flowers, the wax begonia has become one of the most popular bedding plants in America.

The soil should be allowed to dry out between waterings. Fertilize these plants heavily.

Hybridizers have had a field day with begonias, and a profuse array of new varieties appears yearly. All bear glossy, waxy leaves and flowers from May until frost.

For information on *Tuberous Begonia*, see *Color in the Shade*, page 24.

Bergenia; Heart-Leaf Bergenia

Ground cover
Dense to light shade
Hardy to Zone 2

Because of its bold evergreen foliage, its toughness, and its ability to grow happily in almost any exposure, even deep shade, bergenia is a basic plant for the shade garden. Its most common uses are as drifts of ground cover for small to medium-sized areas, as a rock garden subject, as edging, and as a clumping accent in any shaded area.

Its ¾-inch spring flowers, white to rose-pink, appear in tight, nosegaylike clusters atop stems 6 to 12 inches above foliage.

The leaves, 12 to 16 inches high and up to 10 inches wide (cabbagelike or water lily-like), create useful contrasts with smaller-textured ground covers, taller bedding plants, and shrubs. They are wavy-edged and more or less heart-shaped at the base.

Any but very light soils suit this adaptable plant, although excessively moist, fertile soil necessitates frequent division. It is quite drought-tolerant once established. Fair to good drainage, some shade, and protection from heavy winds are the only requirements for situating it properly. Space plants 10 to 18 inches apart. It is unsuited to desert climates.

In most respects bergenia can be neglected with impunity, although it needs protection from snails and slugs, which it harbors. If clumps become crowded or rhizomes leggy, divide them in the fall or early spring.

'Perfecta', a new horticultural variety, is tall and robust. It produces rosy red flowers on strong stems. The foliage of *B. c. purpurea* changes color dramatically in the fall, to purple with crimson highlights.

B. crassifolia (Winter-Blooming Bergenia) grows slightly taller than *B. cordifolia*, to around 20 inches. Leaves are slightly smaller, and in the autumn they color more vividly. Lilac, reddish pink, or purple flowers appear in dense clusters in January and February.

Browallia 'Heavenly Bells'

BROWALLIA SPECIOSA

Sapphire flower
Annual
Dense to light shade

The sapphire flower is one of the exclusive club of shade-tolerant annuals. Still relatively undiscovered by the gardening public, these low-growing jewels deserve wider use. Most varieties will trail, but some are dwarf and compact. Plant them for a cool blue carpet under the filtered shade of trees or on the sunny east side of the house. Let them cascade over a wall or trickle from baskets under the eaves or lathes.

Plant in rich, well-drained soil. Shade is best. Flowers will fade in full sun. Keep the soil evenly moist and make frequent applications of a light fertilizer. Cut plants back in the fall and bring them inside, where they will bloom all winter.

BRUNNERA MACROPHYLLA

Siberian Bugloss
Perennial
Light shade to full sun
Hardy to Zone 3

The tiny flowers of Siberian bugloss, produced in delicate clusters, resemble those of *Anchusa azurea*, the Italian bugloss. This plant, however, has the advantage of large, heart-shaped leaves that remain attractive all season long. This very adaptable plant performs well in any soil, in sun or shade, although light shade is best. Like most garden plants, however, it responds best to moist soil that is high in organic matter. Space plants 12 to 18 inches apart.

The flower color is a clear sky blue, and blooms appear generously in branching, open clusters

Buxus sempervirens

atop stems 12 to 15 inches tall. They bloom in April through May, and somewhat resemble forget-me-nots. The dark green leaves are clean, lush, and pest-free. They reach 6 to 8 inches long in July and grow in basal clumps about 12 inches high. The foliage is attractive until frost.

The plant expands outward gradually. It is well behaved, not invasive, and lives a long time without requiring division.

BUXUS SEMPERVIRENS

Common Boxwood
Broad-leafed evergreen shrub
Medium shade to full sun
Hardy to Zone 6

Shaped as globes and cubes and teddy bears, this is the plant most commonly used in formal gardens to shear into fantastic shapes. Besides topiary and trimmed hedges, the common boxwood also makes an uncommonly beautiful specimen in old age, since it grows quite slowly into a gnarled, spreading, and open treelike shrub, 10 to 20 feet in height and width. Most of us know it as a young plant, however, when it is a dainty, rounded, compact shrub. It does not do well in extremes of heat and cold, and is subject to a wide variety of insect and disease pests.

Plant boxwood in well-drained, moist soil that has been generously amended with organic matter, and mulch heavily to provide a cool, moist root run. Each year prune out the inner dead twigs and remove the fallen leaves that accumulate in the branch crotches. This will help prevent twig canker disease, which is common in the East. Never cultivate around boxwoods, because they root close to the surface. They will not tolerate drought. Protect them from drying winds and extreme temperatures, and give them medium shade in hot climates, medium shade to full sun elsewhere. Many cultivars are available for increased hardiness and different forms and sizes. 'Northern Find' and 'Vardar Valley' are two of the hardiest (to Zone 5).

Buxus microphylla (Littleleaf Boxwood) is similar to the common boxwood, except that it is slightly hardier and more finely textured, and its foliage usually turns yellow-brown in cold weather. However, 'Tide Hill', 'Wintergreen', and others are cultivars of *Buxus microphylla* var. *koreana* (Korean Boxwood) that are hardy to Zone 5 and retain their excellent green foliage all winter long. Cultural instructions and landscape uses are the same as for common boxwood.

Caltha palustris

CALADIUM

For information on *Caladium*, see *Color in the Shade*, page 18.

CALTHA PALUSTRIS

Marsh Marigold
Perennial
Light shade to full sun
Hardy to Zone 3

The marsh marigold is a cheerful little plant for wet, soggy soil or standing water. It has bright golden yellow flowers about 1 inch across borne singly above the foliage. The bright green, rounded leaves are held horizontally on tall, juicy stems. A spring bloomer (May), the entire plant disappears by midsummer.

The plant is fairly low growing, from 12 to 18 inches high. Although not considered invasive, it will expand to form loose clumps and mats. It reseeds if conditions are favorable. Plants bloom the third year from seed.

Marsh marigold needs rich soil that is high in organic matter and with a constant moisture supply. With abundant watering the plant will tolerate drier soils. It grows happily in marshy areas or standing water. Give it light shade to full sun. Plant 12 to 24 inches apart.

Care is moderately easy to moderately difficult. Water abundantly and fertilize regularly. Mulch well if it is planted in exposed, dry locations. There are no serious pests. Divide to increase just after blooming is over. The plant can go for years without needing division.

Calycanthus floridus

Campanula carpatica

Cercis canadensis

CALYCANTHUS FLORIDUS

**Carolina Allspice,
Strawberry Shrub**
Deciduous shrub
Light shade to medium sun
Hardy to Zone 5

For fragrance in bloom and easy care, the Carolina allspice is hard to beat. Plant it wherever you can enjoy the fragrance—near outdoor living areas, under windows, beside screen doors, in the shrub border. The 2-inch, dull, reddish brown flowers gloriously permeate the garden with a sweet strawberry scent in mid-May, and often sporadically into July. The shrub grows slowly to a neat, rounded outline, 6 to 9 feet high and 6 to 12 feet wide. It will grow in any soil, but performs best in deep, moist loam. It prefers light shade, and will not grow as tall in full sun. The shrub transplants readily and is highly resistant to pests. Prune after flowering.

Calycanthus fertilis (Pale Sweetshrub; Hardy to Zone 6), and *Calycanthus occidentalis* (California Sweetshrub; Hardy to Zone 7), are similar species that are occasionally mistaken for Carolina allspice, but they do not have the latter's pleasing floral fragrance. Since fragrance is the chief motive for acquiring *Calycanthus floridus*, purchase it while it is in flower to ensure positive identification.

CAMELLIA

For information on *Camellia*, see *Color in the Shade*, page 19.

CAMPANULA MEDIUM

Canterbury Bells
Biennial grown as an annual
Light shade to full sun

Dangling their loose, open clusters of bell-shaped flowers atop waving leafy stems, Canterbury bells are perfect for the informal garden where a soft, natural look is desired. Plant them about the rock garden in small groups or across a sunny meadow in a broad swath. Mix them into the cottage garden or mass them in waves in the border. They will behave best planted in dense groups, where they can help support each other's 12 to 36-inch flexible stems. (You may still have to stake them in windy spots.) They bloom from June through July, in white and shades of blue, lavender, and pink.

Canterbury bells need rich, moist, well-drained soil. They will accept light shade to full sun. Plant them 4 to 12 inches apart. Keep the soil evenly moist.

Several forms of this biennial are offered as "annual" strains, but even these should be started well in advance to ensure flowering the first year. Many nurseries offer young plants for sale. Canterbury bells are likely to reseed, which increases their desirability in naturalized gardens.

CAMPANULA PERSICIFOLIA

Peach-Leaf Bellflower
Perennial
Light shade to full sun
Hardy to Zone 3

The blue or white blossoms of the peach-leaf bellflower are a charming addition to any wild garden or informal border.

The flowers are bell-shaped, single or double, and spread open to 1½ inches in diameter. They appear in July on long, slender, flexible stems. The leaves are medium green and straplike and, as indicated by the common name, are similar to those of the peach tree.

The plant spreads outward gradually. It is restrained in growth, not invasive, and can be quite long-lived. As bellflower is native to mountainous meadows and open woods, the soil must be well drained, and should be high in organic matter and of average fertility. Give the plant medium shade to full sun. It does best in areas with cool summers, and does not perform well in the South. Space plants 12 to 18 inches apart.

Care is easy. Water regularly, as bellflower does not tolerate prolonged drought. Feed lightly and infrequently. The tallest varieties may require staking, although this is unusual. Crown rot can be a serious problem if water stands around the roots for any length of time. Regular applications of insecticide may be beneficial in protecting the plants from aphids and thrips.

Divide to rejuvenate when the clumps begin to decline, usually not before the third or fourth year. Division in early spring is an excellent means of increase.

Campanula carpatica (Carpathian Harebell) is a low, 6 to 12-inch-tall plant with large blue, purple, or white blossoms from June to August. It is neat, compact, and long-blooming, and is useful in rock gardens, in front of borders, or as an edging. Slugs can be a problem.

CERCIS CANADENSIS

Eastern Redbud
Deciduous tree
Light shade to full sun
Zones 5 to 8

Best known for its pinkish red, pea-shaped flowers that bloom on bare branches in the spring, eastern redbud blooms about the same time as the dogwood; together, they make an attractive combination.

It is a year-round performer, with its green, heart-shaped leaves, yellow fall color, interesting seed pods, and reddish brown bark in winter. It grows fast to 25 or 35 feet in height and an equal width, with an irregular round head and attractive, horizontally tiered branches.

Eastern redbud will grow in light shade or sun, and in acid or alkaline soil. It is an excellent tree on the patio, in a container, or anywhere that space is limited.

'Forest Pansy' has red branches and beautiful purple foliage that is best viewed where the light can shine through. 'Oklahoma', with its dark red flowers and shiny foliage, is the best redbud for high heat and alkaline soils. 'Alba' has white flowers, and is susceptible to fireblight and borers.

Chamaecyparis obtusa 'Spiralis'

Chrysogonum virginianum

Cimicifuga racemosa

CHAMAECYPARIS

False Cypress

Coniferous shrub
Light shade to full sun
Hardiness varies according
to species

While the species are all large trees, each is available in a variety of dwarf cultivars that can be used as coniferous evergreen shrubs. Many *Chamaecyparis* are primarily adapted to moderate and moist coastal climates, while a few perform well in the harsher conditions of the Midwest. Care should be taken to match the selection to the climate.

With evergreen foliage similar to the juvenile leaves of junipers, cultivars vary in foliage color—bright yellows, deep greens, grays, and blues—and habit—from tiny, inches-high tufts to open, picturesque, small trees.

Transplant false cypress into rich, well-drained soil in the spring. Give it full sun in moist, mild climates, and light shade elsewhere. Pruning to control form is best accomplished just before the new foliage emerges in the spring. Most forms have a tendency to die out in the center and lose their lower branches with age. A strong jet of water is the easiest way to remove this foliage. Protect all *Chamaecyparis* from hot, drying winds.

Chamaecyparis lawsoniana (Lawson False Cypress; Zones 6 to 8) is best adapted to coastal, moist climates, and is not suitable for midwestern conditions. Root rot is a significant problem in this species on the West Coast. Yellow-leafed varieties are particularly susceptible to burn by hot sun and drying winds.

Chamaecyparis obtusa (Hinoki False Cypress; Zones 5 to 8)

tolerates neutral soils somewhat better than other false cypresses, and is probably the best choice for midwestern conditions. It is available in a wide variety of dwarf forms.

Chamaecyparis pisifera (Japanese False Cypress; Zones 4 to 8) is the hardiest of the false cypresses, but is notorious for losing its inner and lower foliage with age. It distinctly prefers acid soil.

CHRYSOGONUM
VIRGINIANUM

Golden Star

Perennial
Light shade to full sun
Hardy to Zone 5

Golden star is a low, trailing plant with small, daisylike, bright yellow flowers and vivid green leaves. It is useful either in sun or shade, and is particularly delightful when grown against or around rocks. Chrysogonum must have excellent drainage and prefers a sandy soil high in organic matter. The soil should be fairly dry and of only average fertility. Space plants 8 to 12 inches apart.

The flowers appear in mid-June to frost and are produced along the joints of trailing, leafy stems. The bright green leaves are small and round, about an inch across, and are densely produced. Most varieties sold commercially have gray-green foliage.

The plant has a loose, open habit that follows the contour of the ground and rocks. It usually grows 2 to 4 inches high, and rarely exceeds 8 inches. It often spreads into a loose mat with stems rooting where they touch the soil. Golden star is always restrained in growth and never intrusive, seldom exceeding a spread of 12 to 20 inches.

CIMICIFUGA RACEMOSA

Black Snakeroot, Bugbane

Perennial
Light shade
Hardy to Zone 3

The black snakeroot produces tall, thin, graceful spires of white, fluffy flowers, sometimes reaching 8 feet above the foliage clumps. It is excellent in the rear of the border.

Open and airy in bloom, the wandlike flower stalks sway with each breeze. The flowers are small and are produced densely along the upper part of the stalks in clusters up to 3 feet long. They are vertical and graceful, and exude a cloying sweet fragrance. The peak bloom occurs in late June and July, but small lateral branches bear flowers into August.

The glistening dark green leaves are compound, divided into three-toothed leaflets. The foliage forms dense clumps 2 to 3 feet high and provides good color until frost. Since the plant is native to the deep, rich, moist soils of open woodlands and the forest edge, it does best in moist, well-drained soil high in organic matter. It grows tallest in deep soil and light shade, and ideally should not have more than 4 hours of direct sun each day. In deep shade, however, it will not flower well.

Black snakeroot does not self-sow freely or spread about the garden, and can not be considered intrusive. The rhizomes expand slowly to increase the clump. The plant is long-lived.

CLARKIA

Godetia, Rocky Mountain Garland Flower, Farewell-to-Spring

Annual
Light shade to full sun

In most catalogs the gardener will find "Clarkia" (Rocky Mountain Garland Flower, Farewell-to-Spring) and "Godetia" (sometimes called Farewell-to-Spring also) listed as separate flowers. Indeed, they bear little resemblance to one another, and godetia was formerly a distinct genus; but both are now considered hybrids of species from the same genus, *Clarkia*.

Godetias produce clusters of upward-facing cup or funnel-shaped blossoms with contrasting margins and centers. The flowers, 1 to 3 inches wide, resemble azalea blossoms, and appear on strong stems ideal for cutting. They are widely grown commercially for cut flowers.

Those flowers usually referred to as clarkias concentrate their showy blossoms in the axils, where branches join the main stem. Their blossoms can be

Clethra alnifolia

Clarkia

Clivia miniata

CLETHRA ALNIFOLIA

Summersweet, Sweet Pepperbush
Deciduous shrub
Light shade
Zones 3 to 9

Its extremely fragrant, cool white flower spikes make a welcome addition to the garden in July and August when flowers are scarce. Summersweet is particularly useful in those difficult wet, shady areas of the garden, although it will thrive in nearly any soil. Once established, it will grow slowly to a broad, oval mass 3 to 8 feet high and 4 to 8 feet wide. It is cloaked in handsome, dark green, pest-free foliage that inconsistently turns a clear yellow in the fall before dropping.

Although summersweet is quite tolerant of salty, sandy coastal conditions, its best garden performance is in moist, acid soil that is heavily supplemented with organic matter. It is reputedly difficult to establish. Try planting balled and burlapped or containerized plants in early spring, and water profusely. Although native to swamps, nursery-grown clethras are usually grown in well-drained soils, so that their roots are no longer adapted to swampy soil conditions. When transplanting into wet soils, ease the transition by planting 3 to 4 inches higher than the soil level and mulching heavily. Clethra is intolerant of drought.

Although rarely necessary, pruning should be done in early spring. It is best to allow this shrub to attain its naturally clean, dense, oval shape. The plant will attract great quantities of bees while in flower.

'Paniculata' is a cultivar with longer flowered spikes and is superior to the typical species. 'Rosea' has clear pink buds that open into flowers of white tinged with pink.

CLIVIA MINIATA

Kaffir Lily
Bulb
Dense to light shade

Its foliage is impressive year-round, but the kaffir lily's spring flowers are show-stoppers. It blooms brilliantly in deep shade and even more brilliantly in medium shade.

Umbels of up to 20 flowers atop 12 to 18-inch stems appear in the spring, or earlier if the plant is grown indoors. Some modern hybrids are white or shades of red, salmon, and yellow, although the orange-red, yellowish-centered Victorian favorites are still the most common. Individual flowers are 2 to 3 inches wide. Bright red 1-inch berries sometimes follow blooms.

Straplike dark green leaves grow to 20 inches long and 3 inches wide in balanced pairs from the center of the plant. They are substantial, and as graceful as any foliage in the garden.

Clivia can be planted out with various shade plants, but it usually does better in containers for two reasons. Its large, fleshy roots need to be crowded to induce heavy blooming. And, as clivia prefers night temperatures no lower than 50°F, planters can be moved indoors during cool weather. It should be planted with the tuber barely showing above the soil surface and left undisturbed for as many years as possible.

Keep clivia moist. Soil should be allowed to dry just slightly when growth slows in autumn, but not enough that the leaves begin to wilt. Regular light feeding is beneficial, winter through summer.

COLEUS

For information on *Coleus*, see *Color in the Shade*, page 23.

CONVALLARIA MAJALIS

Lily-of-the-Valley
Ground cover
Medium shade to medium sun
Zones 1 to 7

The heady fragrance and pristine, delicate beauty of its flowers account for the popularity of lily-of-the-valley in bridal bouquets and its traditional use as a May Day love gift in France. This deciduous perennial ground cover, 6 to 8 inches high, is effective alone or with ferns, beneath trees or high walls, between shade shrubs, and against the north or east sides of buildings. A tough, tenacious plant, lily-of-the-valley is a useful soil binder. It thrives in all but the mildest climates in a wide range of exposures, including medium shade. Every spring it reappears. Plantings enlarge rapidly. From spring until frost it makes a dense, bold-textured carpet.

In midspring, just before its foliage has completely unfurled, it produces delicate stems of ¼-inch, pure white, bell-shaped flowers whose fragrance ranks with that of gardenia, jasmine, and

---

either single or double and look like many tiny ribbons that have been fancifully cut and gathered. Both species reach 18 to 24 inches in height.

Both clarkias and godetias will perform best, and flower the longest, in regions where the summers are dry and cool. They bloom, in shades of pink, purple, red, and white, from summer to frost in optimum climates, for a shorter time where summers are hot and wet. In their native habitat they complete their life cycle on the gradually decreasing moisture from stored winter rain or snow melt. In the South and hot-summer regions of the East and Midwest, the protection of light shade and successive plantings 30 days apart may help to achieve a longer bloom season.

Both clarkias and godetias are musts for any cutting garden, but they are also excellent choices for large beds, mixed borders, and planter boxes. Their requirement for perfectly drained soil makes them naturals for the rock garden.

Soil must have excellent drainage and should be light, sandy, and of low fertility. Give these plants light shade to full sun. Clarkia grows well in coastal and high-altitude areas where the nights are cool. Good success, although a shorter season, can also be enjoyed from spring sowing in the plains states. Do not overwater; allow the plants to dry out between waterings.

Convallaria majalis

violet for sweetness. Small fruits may form, but most drop before the mature, red stage.

Because it requires chilling, lily-of-the-valley does not thrive in Zones 8 to 10. It is hardy in all zones. Its exposure and soil requirements are compatible with, but not limited to, those of most rhododendrons and camellias. Ideally it should have a deep, sandy humus, but ordinary garden soil will do as long as drainage is good. In deep shade, blooms are sparse. Plant whole clumps, or space pips (divisions with upright tips) from 2 to 8 inches apart, preferably in the autumn after dormancy.

Keep the soil moist throughout the growing season. For best foliage and blooms, apply well-rotted manure liberally in the fall. Plants may be thinned every few years.

Aside from the species, two varieties are sometimes available. 'Fortins Giant' (often sold as 'Fortune's Giant') is a more robust plant with larger flowers and leaves. *C. m. rubra* is like the species except for its pink flowers.

CORNUS FLORIDA

Flowering Dogwood
Deciduous tree
Light shade
Hardy to Zone 4

In light shade this small (around 20 foot), deciduous tree creates a beautiful understory. It is brilliant with blossoms in spring, lush through summer, ablaze with autumn color, and striking when its layered structure is revealed in winter. Not surprisingly, it is many people's favorite flowering tree. Its growth rate is slow to moderate. Several cultivars and related species offer variety in size, form, color, and adaptation.

Before the leaves of flowering

Cornus florida

dogwood appear in spring, buds at the twig tips swell into showy 2 to 4-inch white flowers of four and sometimes six petals. (These "petals" are technically bracts, and the tiny "stamens" at the center of each "flower" are the true flowers.) Glossy scarlet berries in sparse clusters last into winter or until birds have stripped them.

Leaves are dark green ovals to 6 inches long and 3 inches wide; in autumn they turn red or burgundy-red.

Flowering dogwood prefers light shade; in its native habitat it has filtered shade from taller forest trees. Acid well-drained soil is necessary. Roots need moisture and protection from extreme heat. Mulch helps to provide both, and maintains soil acidity as it decays. Branches may be selectively thinned to emphasize structure.

Several varieties of *Cornus florida* are available. Check with your nursery for local hardiness of the different varieties and species. 'Cherokee Chief' has rich rose-red flowers and a fairly upright habit. 'Cherokee Princess' has an abundance of white flowers. 'Cloud 9' produces white flowers early and very profusely. It accepts temperature extremes better than the species. *C. f. pendula* is a weeping form. *C. f. plena* has double white flowers. 'Rainbow' has white flowers, and yellow-and-green leaves that color brilliantly in late summer and early fall. *C. f. welchii* has variegated grayish green leaves with irregular pink-and-white margins.

Related Species

All species grow in light shade, unless another exposure is specified.

C. alba sibirica (Siberian Dogwood) is a 6 or 7-foot shrub with clusters of tiny white flowers and, in cold-winter areas, startling coral-red branches.

C. canadensis (Bunchberry) is a deciduous ground cover 5 to 9 inches high, appropriate for shaded woodland settings. It produces small heads of yellow flowers surrounded by showy white bracts. In late summer and autumn it bears bright red edible berries.

C. kousa (Kousa Dogwood) is sometimes multistemmed, has 2 to 3-inch white flowers with pointed petals, and bears edible fruit. *C. k. chinensis* has larger flowers.

C. mas (Cornelian Cherry) is a slow-growing shrub or small tree bearing small yellow flowers on bare branches in late winter and early spring. Fruit is edible. It will extend branches and flowers from a partially shaded spot into a deeply shaded one.

C. stolonifera (*C. sericea*) (Red-Osier Dogwood) is an extremely hardy shrub that can form a thicket. It accepts constant moisture. Flowers are white, in small clusters. Berries are white or bluish. *C. s.* 'Flaviramea' has red twigs.

C. sessilis (Black-Fruit Dogwood), a large shrub or small tree native to the West Coast, has jade-green foliage, tiny whitish flowers, and shiny black fruit. It will accept lots of wetness and grows well in medium shade.

Cyclamen

CYCLAMEN

Hardy Cyclamen
Perennial
Light shade
Zones 5 to 9

Both the familiar florist's cyclamen and the smaller, less well-known hardy species are native to Mediterranean regions. Florist's cyclamen is generally grown indoors, and will grow outside only in Zones 9 and 10. Here, we are considering only the hardy cyclamen.

Cyclamen foliage is almost as pretty as its flowers. Heart-shaped leaves are often marked in pale green, white, or silver. The teardrop-shaped buds blossom into butterflylike blooms with reflexed petals that turn backward like wings. They hover over the plants on slender brownish red stems.

The hardy cyclamen grows to 4 or 5 inches in height, with ¾ to 1-inch flowers. It grows best in Zones 5 through 9, but can tolerate colder climates if adequately mulched in the winter. Plant tubers in midsummer in light shade and rich soil. It is especially attractive in woodland settings.

Species bloom in the fall or spring. *C. cilicium*, or Sicily cyclamen, bears pale pink flowers against silver-traced leaves in the fall. *C. coum* (*C. atkinsii*) is a spring bloomer with flowers in white, pink, or red. Fall blossoms of the European cyclamen, *C. europaeum*, are rose-red and very fragrant, and the foliage is mottled in silver and white. Marbled foliage is also characteristic of late summer-blooming *C. neapolitanum*, the Neapolitan cyclamen. The rose-pink or white flowers of this fragrant plant bloom before its foliage.

Dennstaedtia punctilobula

Dicentra spectabilis

Digitalis species

DENNSTAEDTIA PUNCTILOBULA

Hay-scented Fern
Fern
Deep shade to full sun
Hardy to Zone 4

The hay-scented fern is native to eastern United States and Canada. The finely cut pinnacles form fronds with a pyramidal outline. These feathery fronds are yellow-green and grow 20 to 32 inches long and 11 inches wide. They smell of freshly cut hay when broken, hence the common name. The fronds are deciduous, turning brown in early fall. This fern adapts to a wide range of growing conditions from deep shade to full sun, and alternately wet and dry seasons. It prefers a slightly acid (pH 5.5 to 6.5), damp soil with a woodland mulch, but will grow in most types of soil. The rhizomes spread rapidly, forming a dense mat just below the soil surface. The hay-scented fern is an excellent ground cover, but should only be planted where it is allowed to spread freely. If it becomes too invasive, pull out the excess rhizomes. These rhizomes can then be planted to establish the fern in another area. The fern is especially effective for erosion control on slopes. Snails and slugs feed on the tender, young foliage and can be controlled with baits commercially available in nurseries.

DICENTRA SPECTABILIS

Bleeding Heart
Perennial
Medium shade to medium sun
Hardy to Zone 2

The flowers of the bleeding heart are aptly named. They are puffy and suggest a heart with two "drops of blood" flaring up and out from the base, resulting in an overall lyre shape. The blossoms are pink, rose-pink with white tips, or occasionally white in color, and hang pendulously from horizontally arching and drooping stems. The flower clusters are up to 9 inches long, and are produced among and on top of the foliage.

The foliage is medium green, often with a slightly graying cast, with deeply cut leaves that give the plant a fine-textured appearance. The plant forms dense clumps of arching sprays of foliage 30 inches tall and up to 36 inches wide. Because of its relatively large size and a tendency to die down after blooming, it is best used as a specimen rather than massed, and used with accompanying plants that will succeed its effect later in the season.

The plant prefers rich, moist, well-drained soil that is high in organic matter. It will tolerate medium shade to full sun; however, in full sun the foliage will burn and die back quickly after flowering. It is also best to keep the plant out of drying winds. Space plants 2 feet apart if not growing as a single specimen.

Dicentra eximia (Fringed Bleeding Heart) is notable for its beautiful gray-green, finely dissected foliage, which contrasts effectively with its deep rose to white flowers. It also has a longer blooming season. Several hybrid forms of this plant (probably crosses with *D. formosa*, among others) will bloom intermittently all summer long if faded blossoms

are removed regularly. One example is the beautiful hybrid 'Bountiful', with intense, deep red flowers off and on from June until frost.

D. formosa (Western Bleeding Heart) is an aggressive spreader with flower stems about 1 foot tall and blossoms rose-purple to white in color.

DIGITALIS PURPUREA

Foxglove
Biennial
Dense to light shade
Hardy to Zone 4

Flowering spikes of foxglove, ranging from purple to white, glow in the darkest hollow of a woodland garden and shine in the back of a shaded bed. Because of its scale (up to 5 feet, sometimes higher) and its innate beauty, foxglove is an imposing flower, and one of the few that will bloom freely in deep shade. It is a biennial, establishing itself the first year and blooming in the late spring and summer of the second. Because it self-sows freely in a suitable spot, it may be considered a perennial—and, by some gardeners, a pretty pest.

The flowers are tubular, to 3 inches long, usually with spotted throats. Flowers of the species are pendulous and cover only one side of the stem. Those of one group of hybrids are dense, evenly distributed around the stem, and held straight outward.

The evergreen leaves are large, rough-textured ovals, dark green above, light green and fuzzy beneath. They are largest and most concentrated at the base of the plant. The leaves are poisonous to humans and animals if

eaten. Digitalis, a medicinal drug, is derived from them.

Foxglove requires rich acid soil, moisture, good drainage, some degree of shade, and shelter from strong wind. Hybrids often adapt to less favorable soils. Space them 12 to 24 inches apart.

Stake plants if necessary. Cutting spikes severely after about half the flowers have finished will spur development of new spikes. Cutting them later may encourage second-year bloom. Snail bait, fungicide for powdery mildew, and insecticides for aphids, mealybugs, and Japanese beetles may be needed.

Hybrids of D. purpurea: Excelsior Hybrids produce dense, undrooping flowers all around the spikes. Colors are white and shades of mauve, pink, yellow, and rose. Height is 5 feet or more. Peak bloom is in June. Some gardeners consider this the choicest group of hybrids.

The slightly pendulous flowers of Foxy Hybrids begin at 18 inches and continue until the plants reach 3 feet.

Hyacinth Hybrids have 3-foot flower heads. Big flowers are mottled with red or brown.

Shirley Hybrids have 3-foot flower heads. Flowers are large and crowded. Many are dotted.

Related species and hybrids: D. grandiflora (D. ambigua) (Yellow Foxglove; Perennial Foxglove) is better considered a biennial than a perennial. In July its 3-foot spikes bear 2-inch pale yellow flowers with blotched throats. *D. × 'Mertonensis'* (Merton's Foxglove) bears large, showy strawberry-colored flowers on 3 to 3½-foot spikes in June and July.

Doronicum cordatum

Leopard's Bane
Perennial
Light shade
Hardy to Zone 4

The spring-blooming, daisylike, bright yellow flowers of leopard's bane appear in great quantities above clusters of large, heart-shaped leaves. Each blossom is 2 to 3 inches across and appears on its own 9 to 15-inch stem. The plant blooms in May, and the foliage declines and often dies down after blooming is complete. The foliage is of medium to coarse texture and is produced in low basal clumps of 3 to 5-inch leaves that are medium to bright green in color. The clumps grow 8 to 12 inches high, and with flowers the plant often reaches 2 to 3 feet in height, spreading nearly as wide.

Leopard's bane produces shallow, dense, fibrous roots. The clumps expand rapidly and start dying out in the center unless divided. Because the foliage dies out early in the season, the plant is best used as a specimen rather than massed, and should be combined with other plants that will fill in the empty space. In warm climates with long, mild autumns, the foliage may come back and again produce blooms.

The plant needs rich moist soil that is high in organic matter. It prefers light shade, especially in hot climates. Space plants 12 to 15 inches apart. Water moderately during the growing season. There are no serious pests. Division for rejuvenation is usually required every 2 to 4 years, and is best done during dormancy in August or very early spring. Division is an excellent means of increase.

Dryopteris species

Wood Fern, Shield Fern
Fern
Dense to medium shade
Hardy to Zone 3

This large group of ferns includes many that are native to the forests of the United States and Canada. Most are very hardy, evergreen, and easy to grow.

All wood ferns need shade, moist soil, and a humus-rich soil. Many forms spread by underground runners, and so are easily propagated by division.

D. austriaca spinulosa, the florist's fern, is widely distributed throughout eastern North America. Its fronds are harvested in summer and shipped in winter.

A good landscape accent plant also native to the Northeast is the leather wood fern, *D. marginalis*. It grows in clumps to about 2 feet high and is hardy to −35°F.

The coastal wood fern, *D. arguta*, is native to western North America. It grows to about 3 feet.

Indian Strawberry, Mock Strawberry
Perennial
Medium to light shade
Hardy to Zone 4

This evergreen strawberry relative and lookalike is a versatile ground cover. Although in most areas it accepts sun, it is more at home in medium to light shade. It grows sparsely in deep shade. Once established it tolerates drought with no lessening of attractiveness, but it thrives with moisture as well. The flowers are pretty, and the berries resemble strawberries. Like strawberries, the Indian strawberry spreads by runners, but more rapidly, to form a dense mat about 6 inches high, sometimes higher in heavy shade. It can cover medium to large areas. Its flowers, berries, and graceful runners make it a useful subject for hanging baskets.

Bright yellow flowers, ½ to 1 inch across, are held conspicuously above the foliage. They are followed by ½-inch scarlet berries, tasteless to birds as well as to people, so they remain to brighten the garden for weeks. The leaves, on slender stems, are composed of three soft-green leaflets, more textured and less glossy than strawberry foliage.

Any well-drained soil suits *Duchesnia*. It mats more densely in bright areas than in dark ones. Plant at 12 to 18-inch intervals. Occasional foot traffic is all right. Hardier than strawberry, it is indifferent to neglect. Because it spreads rapidly, it can be a nuisance, although an easily controlled one.

Duchesnia indica

Purple Coneflower
Perennial
Light shade to full sun
Hardy to Zone 3

The purple coneflower is a large, coarse plant with daisylike flowers that have relaxed, drooping "petals." Named varieties are much superior to the species.

The flowers come in purple and, occasionally, white varieties. The "petals," technically ray flowers, droop back toward the stem. The eye is conical, bristly, and colored purple, maroon, or brown. The flowers are 3 to 4 inches wide and appear at the ends of many long, branched stems. They bloom in July to September. The foliage is dull green and composed of large, coarse-textured leaves that are dense at the base of the plant, smaller and more scattered toward the top. The plant forms a clump of many stems, which are branched, semierect, and spreading.

Purple coneflower grows 3 to 5 feet high and 2 to 5 feet wide. It is long-lived and not invasive. The soil should be sandy and well drained. The plant prefers light shade, which produces richer colors than does full sun. It is native to North American prairies and meadows, mostly at the edges of woods. It is drought and wind-tolerant. Space plants 18 to 24 inches apart.

Purple coneflower responds to light feeding and moderate watering. Never allow the soil to remain soggy. Japanese beetles can

Epimedium

Erythronium

Euonymus species

ruin this plant very quickly; protect it with traps or insecticide. Clumps will require division every third or fourth year for rejuvenation. This is also an excellent means of increase, and should be performed in early spring as new growth appears.

It is best to purchase named varieties, as most have bigger flowers and better color than the species.

'The King' is probably the most famous hybrid. Its 6-inch flowers are a brilliant reddish purple with brown centers. It grows to 3 feet, and has a more refined appearance than does the species.

'White Lustre' has creamy white flowers that are produced in incredible profusion, even in severe drought. Its foliage and structure, however, are quite coarse.

EPIMEDIUM

Barrenwort, Bishop's-Hat
Ground cover
Dense shade to full sun
Hardy to Zone 3

The epimediums are easy to grow, hardy, and too seldom used. They spread with creeping roots to make a uniform, 9-inch ground cover. The plant is semi-evergreen; most of the leathery, heart-shaped leaves die back in winter but a few last into January. In early spring, the new leaves are pale green with some rose color. During midseason they are a deep, glossy green and in fall they turn reddish. Tiny ½-inch orchidlike flowers (shaped like a bishop's hat) appear in May. Many colors are available and they last

well when cut. Epimediums are very hardy, tolerating temperatures to − 40°F.

They are long-lived and easy to grow. Light shade is usually best, but they will tolerate full sun if the soil (preferably acidic) is rich and moist. They will tolerate deep shade if drainage is good, although flower production will suffer. The creeping roots are close to the surface, so don't cultivate around them. Planted 10 inches apart, they will fill in without overcrowding. To propagate, divide the clumps in early spring. Cut off old leaves so that small flowers and new leaves will be visible.

Epimediums thrive in the light shade of other acid-soil plants such as the taller rhododendrons, camellias, and ferns. Their roots compete well with others, so epimediums are ideal for planting under trees and shrubs.

E. grandiflorum is the most commonly cultivated form. It grows to about a foot. 'Rose Queen' has the bright, rose-colored flowers with white-tipped spurs. The hybrid *E. versicolor* 'Sulphureum' has yellow flowers. *E. youngianum* 'Niveum' grows compactly and has white flowers.

ERYTHRONIUM

Erythronium
Bulb
Medium shade to medium sun
Hardiness varies according to species

This picturesque group comes mainly from North American woodlands, although the one European native, *E. dens-canis*, is the

best known. Its common name, dog-tooth violet, has nothing to do with the appearance of the flower, but is based on the resemblance of the corm to a dog's tooth. The delicate flower is purple or rose colored, rising from mottled leaves on a 6-inch stem. It is hardy to Zone 3.

A number of species, many of them with mottled foliage, are American natives. They are known by several descriptive names, most commonly fawn lily, trout lily, adder's-tongue, and Easter bells. *E. grandiflorum* (hardy to Zone 6) has plain green foliage and 24-inch stems with yellow blossoms. *E. citrinum* also bears yellow flowers, but the stems are only 8 inches tall.

The other species grow to a height of about 12 inches with flower colors as follows: *E. albidum* (hardy to Zone 5), white to light blue; *E. americanum* (hardy to Zone 4), yellow tinged with pink; *E. californicum*, creamy white or yellow; *E. hendersonii*, purple; *E. oregonum*, creamy white; *E. revolutum*, creamy to purple; and *E. tuolumnense*, yellow with a greenish base. All bloom in the spring, and many have a delicate fragrance. The latter five are all hardy to Zone 6.

Plant in medium to light shade in warm areas, or in medium sun where summers are cooler. Plant in the fall in moist, well-drained soil. Erythronium will

need moisture all summer long even though dormant, and it does not like extreme heat. Fall mulching offers sufficient protection in cold regions. It is especially attractive in a woodland setting.

EUONYMUS FORTUNEI

Wintercreeper
Evergreen vine or prostrate shrub
Medium shade to full sun
Zones 5 to 8

Hardy, tough wintercreeper grows in nearly every part of North America, in virtually any soil or exposure. Flowers are inconspicuous, but evergreen foliage of this species and its varieties is attractive, even striking, and dependably fresh looking. It is a vine or prostrate shrub used as a ground cover. Stems root wherever they touch moist soil, spreading out to 4 feet, sometimes much farther, and forming a dense mass up to 2 feet high. When well established, it leaves no room for weeds. Deep roots bind soil on slopes or banks. It will cover rocky soil and stumps, fill in solidly under shrubs and trees, and serve as a lawn substitute in shade. Roots cling to rough surfaces, enabling wintercreeper to climb to 20 feet or more. It grows well everywhere except in desert areas. Even there, it sometimes succeeds reasonably well. It prefers medium

Festuca ovina glauca

shade to full sun. In dense shade, where the climate is cool, mildew is a problem.

Care is easy, unless infested by scale. Dormant oil spray in early spring, followed by applications of diazinon or Orthene when the orange-red crawlers appear, will kill scale.

The species itself is less popular than these varieties: 'Coloratus' (Purpleleaf Wintercreeper), the most popular, turns various shades of purple during autumn and winter. It forms a dense, even carpet 6 to 10 inches high and is a vigorous grower.

'Gricilis', smaller and less vigorous than 'Coloratus', has white or yellowish variegated leaves that turn rosy in winter.

'Kewensis' (Kew Wintercreeper), sometimes sold as 'Minimus', is a dwarf about 2 inches high. The ¼-inch-long leaves have near-white veins. It is appropriate as a ground cover or rock garden subject.

'Radicans' is the fastest growing of the small-leaf varieties, making quick ground or wall cover. It is confusing that the species, *E. fortunei*, is sometimes sold as *E. radicans*—not the same as diminutive cultivar *E. fortunei* 'Radicans'.

FATSIA JAPONICA

Japanese Aralia
Evergreen shrub
Dense to medium shade
Hardy to Zone 7

Japanese aralia is also listed as *Aralia japonica* or *A. sieboldiana*. The gardener faced with a deeply shaded entryway, an overhung north wall, an empty container in a recessed spot, or any other deep-shade problem situation that calls for bold greenery should consider this easy solution. Japanese aralia, a close relative of

the common ivies, can create a luxurious tropical effect in the darkest, most discouraging corner of the garden. And it is one of the easiest shade plants to grow. A single plant can quickly fill an area 6 to 8 feet high and as wide, and in time an even larger area, with handsome evergreen foliage and occasional blooms and fruit.

The blooms, which appear in the fall and winter, are rather uninteresting individually but showy in their compound milky white clusters up to 18 inches long. Round black berries, to ¼ inch in diameter, last through the winter.

The leaves are deeply lobed, roundish, to 16 inches wide, and held on 12-inch stems. They are dark green and glossy.

Any spot in dense or medium shade that is sheltered from the wind is good. Virtually any soil is acceptable, although rich, moist, acid soil is best. Fertilize periodically. If the leaves are yellowish with dark green veins, supplement feeding with chelated iron or iron sulfate. As plants begin to lose their lower leaves, prune low to encourage sprouting from the base. If space allows, plant one or more smaller plants in front of an older, larger one. Watch for snails and slugs, and hose off aphids.

'Moseri' is low and compact. 'Variegata' has leaves with golden or creamy borders.

FESTUCA OVINA GLAUCA

Dwarf Blue Fescue
Ground cover
Light shade to full sun
Hardy to Zone 4

This is a popular, small, tufted grass with finely textured, silvery blue evergreen foliage. It grows from 6 to 12 inches high in a neat

Fragaria chiloensis

mound. It must have well-drained soil, and prefers light shade or full sun. Frequent division is required or the center of the clump will die out, especially in moist, rich soil. Removing the flowers as they appear prolongs its useful life. In Southern California, festuca is one of the few gray plants that will do well with light shade. Its color is better without the browning at the tips sometimes caused by the sun.

FRAGARIA CHILOENSIS

Wild or Sand Strawberry
Perennial
Light shade
Hardy to Zone 5

Rich, glossy foliage, not fruit, is this evergreen perennial's greatest asset in the garden. In light shade it makes a deep-green ground cover for large or small areas, including slopes, and a filler for the front of beds. Its runners trail gracefully over walls and banks. It will grow in medium shade, but sparsely and with dull, not glossy, leaves.

Inch-wide white flowers appear in spring (late winter in coastal areas). In the wild, red berries develop in spring and summer. Wild strawberry seldom fruits in the garden, and when it does the berries are usually dry and tasteless.

Leaves vary in size, depending on soil and climate. Usually each leaflet of the three-part leaf is 2 inches long. Leaves form a mat from 6 to 10 inches high.

In its native habitat, wild strawberry grows in sandy soil, sometimes covering dunes. In the garden it likes similar soil, sandy and fast-draining. Plant it from flats or sections of runners, spaced a foot or more apart. In early spring, clip or mow plants. If after 2 or 3 years the cover becomes sparse and uneven, rake the area vigorously in early spring to thin old growth and stimulate new. Then fertilize lightly with lawn fertilizer. Wild strawberry requires average watering in light shade, infrequent watering in deeper shade. Infestations of spider mites can be controlled by spraying.

Rancho Santa Ana Botanic Garden in California has developed Hybrid Ornamental Strawberry No. 25, a larger plant and more vigorous grower, which produces delicious berries. It is virtually free of disease except for some mildew when it is overwatered in damp coastal areas.

F. californica (California Wood Strawberry; Hardy to Zone 7) is sometimes available on the West Coast. It is best used in woodland plantings, not as ground cover, in light to medium shade. Moderate to infrequent watering is best.

F. virginiana (Virginia Strawberry; Hardy to Zone 4), native to eastern North America, is occasionaly available in specialty nurseries there. Its uses are similar to those of *F. californica* but it requires more moisture.

Fritillaria species

Gaultheria procumbens

Hakonechloa macra

FRITILLARIA MELEAGRIS

Snake's Head Lily, Checkered Lily, Guinea Hen Flower
Bulb
Light shade
Zones 3 to 8

This hardy European bulb grows to about a foot, sometimes higher, and bears curious but exquisite flowers in a solitary, pendulous habit. In a lightly shaded border, near the edge of a woodland, or in a shaded rock garden it creates a subtle but striking focal point during its April-to-May blooming. If it is well placed, it will naturalize.

Flowers are 2-inch bells on slender stems. Its remarkable coloration and patterning account for its various common names, as it is subtly checkered in purples and maroons, yellow, and white.

Light shade and deep, moist, fast-draining rich soil are best. It particularly likes to grow in unmowed grass, perhaps because there its roots are cooled. It may also be grown in containers. Maintain moisture, and guard against alkalinity where it is a problem by proper mulching and fertilizing.

Several North American species of this genus rank among the most beautiful of American wildflowers, and are well worth locating and cultivating in the woodland garden. Like the calochortuses, they are disappearing from

many areas where they were numerous, but commercial propagation, even if limited, makes these beauties available to the gardener who seeks out unusual and particularly pleasing flowers.

F. lanceolata (Checker Lily, Mission Bells, Hardy to Zone 5), native to California and northwestern North America, bears 1½-inch bell-shaped flowers, chocolate brown to purple, mottled with greenish yellow. Flowers are borne atop a 1 to 3-foot purplish stem with whorls of rich green foliage. Blooming begins in February. It requires friable, fast-draining soil, perhaps composed of leaf mold, peat, and sand. It prefers light shade and moisture, but water should be withheld after blooming for the duration of summer and early fall. Sometimes it naturalizes in a woodland setting.

F. pudica (Yellow Bells; Hardy to Zone 3), less than a foot high, grows in dry, rocky soil in the Rocky Mountains and the Sierra Nevada. It is especially suited to rock garden and container culture.

F. recurva (Scarlet Fritillary; Hardy to Zone 6), native to lightly shaded areas in California and southern Oregon, is the showiest native fritillary. In habit and flower form it resembles _F. lanceolata_, except that its flowers are scarlet, flecked yellow inside the bells and purple-tinged out-

side. Petals curve outward at the tips. Blooming begins in March. Like the other native fritillaries, this one is best planted in the fall, and like them it grows best in California, the Northwest, or wherever the climate is similar.

FUCHSIA

For information on _Fuchsia_, see _Color in the Shade_, page 22.

GAULTHERIA PROCUMBENS

Wintergreen, Teaberry, Checkerberry
Ground cover
Dense to light shade
Hardy to Zone 3

Best known for the flavoring extracted from it, wintergreen is one of the densest evergreen ground covers for dense, medium, or light shade. A single plant spreads by underground stems to form a 3 to 6-inch-high mat covering a square yard.

Its ¼ to ½-inch flowers, resembling lily-of-the-valley flowers but often pink-tinged, appear in May or early summer. The aromatic, scarlet berries that follow last through winter unless eaten by birds, people, or field mice.

Oval leaves, 1 to 2 inches long,

cluster toward the ends of upright stems. Their tops are a glossy dark green, and their undersides light green. In autumn some leaves remain green and others turn orange, crimson, or bronze.

Rich, moist, acid soil and some shade are best for wintergreen. It is useful in woodland gardens, in rock gardens, and in the foreground of borders. Plant in clumps, or set individual plants 12 to 18 inches apart.

Water and weed until well established. A light sprinkling of fine conifer needles or other mulch from time to time will keep soil acidic. Established plants can tolerate some drought, but look better with regular watering.

G. ovatifolia (Western Teaberry, Oregon Wintergreen) is an attractive but seldom available spreading ground cover to 8 inches high. It is similar to wintergreen, except that its leaves are thicker and more serrated, its blossoms are smaller, and it flowers later (June and July).

G. shallon (Salal) is the largest of the gaultherias used in American gardens; it grows to around 5 feet high in a moist shaded location, or 1 to 1½ feet in a dry, bright exposure. Rich green,

Hamamelis × intermedia

Hedera helix

leathery, evergreen leaves, to 5 inches long and 1½ inches wide, are used as greenery by florists. Flowers are like those of *G. procumbens* but larger, on reddish stems in 5 to 6-inch loose clusters. The ¼-inch berries are edible but bland, very attractive to birds. Salal grows in light to medium shade. It tolerates poor soil and drought, although it looks better in rich, well-drained, acid soil. It is a suitable cover beneath trees that tolerate little summer water. It is not yet widely available beyond the West Coast of the United States.

HAKONECHLOA MACRA 'AUREO-VARIEGATA'

Ground cover
Light shade
Hardy to Zone 4

This grass is a relatively recent introduction to the United States from the mountains and forests of Japan. The long, deciduous, arching leaves are variegated creamy white. The plant spreads slowly by rhizomes, and is never invasive. Equally effective in pots or planted in large drifts, the plant presents a neat, uniform appearance, reaching up to 12 inches high. Grow this grass in acid soil that has both excellent drainage and plenty of organic matter. Bright indirect light is best; full sun is not recommended.

HAMAMELIS × INTERMEDIA

Hybrid Witch Hazel
Deciduous shrub
Light shade
Zones 6 to 8

All witch hazels are delightful for their spicily fragrant, delicately showy winter flowers. During periods of extreme cold the flower petals curl up into a tight ball, and thus can withstand prolonged periods covered with ice in 0°F weather. While this hybrid is not as fragrant or as restrained in size as some others, it is the showiest of all the witch hazels available in the United States. As early as February its leafless branches are covered with deep yellow blossoms that last about a month. The red-flowered cultivars, such as 'Jelena' (which is actually a coppery orange), while interesting, are not as outstanding from a distance as are the ones with yellow flowers. This is not a shrub for small gardens—it will eventually reach 15 to 20 feet in height with a comparable spread. Expect an outstanding show of fall color in reds, oranges, and yellows before the leaves drop.

Plant witch hazels in deep, rich soil that has an abundant supply of moisture. While they will not tolerate drought, they don't need to be pampered—they are virtually pest free. Use them as screens, backgrounds, or large focal points, or train them into small trees. Because witch hazels perform well in filtered shade, they make an excellent choice for a naturalized woodland understory. Consider planting them near windows, where their winter blooms can be seen from indoors on a cold day.

Hamamelis vernalis (Vernal Witch Hazel; Zones 6 to 9) has a neat, small habit (6 to 10 feet high and usually much wider) that is round and dense. Powerfully fragrant small yellow flowers appear in January and February. The leaves turn a clear yellow in the fall. It is native to gravelly, often-flooded stream banks in the Ozark mountains.

Hamamelis virginiana (Common Witch Hazel; Zones 5 to 9) is the hardiest but also the largest and rangiest of the witch hazels, growing 20 to 30 feet high and wide. Its yellow flowers in November and December often coincide with the clear yellow fall foliage, reducing their effectiveness, but they are quite fragrant. It is native to forest understories from Canada to Georgia and west to Nebraska.

HEDERA

Ivy
Vine
Dense shade to partial sun
Hardy to Zone 5

As a ground cover, ivy does almost everything: stays green the entire year, spreads rapidly, lies flat, climbs and covers, prevents erosion, provides insulation, works in sun or shade, adapts to most climates, requires minimal care, is easily propagated, and—besides all that—can be enormously attractive.

An ivy bed is most easily begun with well-established plants, which can be purchased in pots. Fast-growing cultivars should be planted one per square foot; small-leaved or slow-growing ivies, two, three, or four to the square foot. Generally, self-branching and compact growers will cover more densely.

Ivy requires well-draining soil and, contrary to popular belief, it prefers high light intensity. It grows best in indirect light, but once established will tolerate full sun or even fairly heavy shade. In deep shade, however, ivy will survive, but growth will be slow.

After the initial growth—ivy spurts in the spring and fall—you can replenish or extend your ivies by taking cuttings. Ivies will grow well despite adverse conditions. They root easily, even in water.

Maintenance of the ivy bed is also easy. It is a good practice to mow it every other year just before the new growth, with the mower at the highest setting. This prevents the growth from becoming so dense that it can harbor such undesirable animal life as snails, slugs, and rats. The plants will be covered with leaves with the first growth of spring.

Watch for leaf spot, which begins as ¼-inch brown or black spots. This condition is generally not serious, but it can become unsightly. If it does, spray the area with a fungicide containing copper. In hot, dry regions care includes watering beds of ivy as much as you would a lawn.

The species *H. helix* has the most cultivars, due mainly to ivy's penchant for sporting—making spontaneous changes in its genetic makeup. In sporting, a plant will suddenly and for no apparent reason produce leaves that differ from the original ones in color, shape, size, or growth pattern.

The berries of *H. helix* are somewhat poisonous.

Helleborus orientalis

HELLEBORUS NIGER

Christmas Rose
Evergreen perennial
Light shade
Hardy to Zone 3; Evergreen
to Zone 5

Christmas rose produces splendid flowers, often out of the snow, sometime between November and March or April. Its substantial, glossy foliage enlivens otherwise drab garden areas during the bleakest months. Not a rose but a relative of the buttercup, it forms drifts of ground cover. Its clumps enlarge by spreading rhizomes, but are slow-growing and never invasive. It is also useful as a specimen or a foreground planting with border shrubs, and it can be used in scattered groupings in woodland gardens.

The flowers, 2 to 4 inches wide, resemble single roses and are usually pure white with bright yellow stamens. Some forms are pinkish or greenish, or become pinkish green or purple as they age. They usually last for several months. The uncommonly handsome leaves are divided into seven or more glossy, dark leaflets, finely serrated toward the tips. The plant is bitter-tasting, and very poisonous to humans and animals.

Christmas rose accepts most rich soils but prefers well-drained neutral or slightly alkaline soil with high organic content.

Care is moderately easy as long as the plant is properly situated and kept moist. Fertilizer is not usually necessary, or even desirable, as nitrogen can damage the roots. Occasional leaf spot fungus is easily treated. This plant dislikes being moved, but if division is necessary, it should be done in the spring, after blooming. The roots should be separated carefully so each division has several eyes (leaf buds). Eyes should be buried about an inch.

H. foetidus (Stinking Hellebore), despite its forbidding name, is a graceful 1½-foot plant with lush, shining, compound leaves that are usually semievergreen. From January to April it produces a profusion of pendulous, bell-shaped, 1-inch blooms, greenish on the lower parts of the plant and reddish higher up. It is drought-tolerant and looks good in planters as well as in the garden situations described for *H. niger.*

H. lividus corsicus (Corsican Hellebore), from Corsica and the Balearic Islands, grows to 2 to 3 feet in height. In late winter or early spring it produces masses of large apple-green flowers that persist until summer. This is the best hellebore for the Southwest and similar climate areas. Like *H. foetidus* it is drought-tolerant when established. This species is hardy to Zone 7.

H. orientalis (Lenten Rose), from Greece and Asia Minor, is the best hellebore for the Southeast. (Actually, several forms are sold under this name. Most have leaves that die during coldest winter, although flowers appear in early to midspring.) It closely resembles *H. niger,* but its foliage is lighter green. Flowers may be deep red, purplish green, pink, or white. All are spotted in shades of green. Cultural requirements are essentially those of *H. niger.*

Hemerocallis 'Valiant'

HEMEROCALLIS

Daylily
Perennial
Light shade to full sun
Hardy to Zone 3

Daylilies are long-lasting perennials with attractive foliage and showy flowers, and are very easy to grow. The individual blossoms last only a day, but are produced continuously over a long season.

Daylilies come in many colors, with flowers in shades of cream, yellow, orange, red, pink, and violet; they are often striped and bicolored. Individually they are from 3 to 5 inches long, and open just as wide. They appear at the ends of long stems. Some varieties are deliciously fragrant. Flowering generally lasts 3 to 4 weeks, but varies according to the cultivar. The bloom season is commonly divided into *early* (late May and June), *middle* (July), and *late* (August into September), although considerable overlapping occurs.

The bright green, handsome, straplike leaves grow 1 to 2 feet long, and are effective all season. The leaves arch out from the base of the plant, forming a mound of foliage. Stems and flowers arise from this mound.

Depending on variety, daylilies can reach from 20 inches to 3 or 4 feet tall, including flowers. They all form a tough, heavy, tuberous root system. Some varieties are evergreen in mild climates.

Daylilies are long-lived, and clumps will expand indefinitely. They are restrained in growth, permanent, not invasive, and compete well with the roots of trees and shrubs. Hybrids will not reseed.

Hemerocallis 'So Big'

Daylilies are highly adaptable, but perform best in well-drained soil that is high in organic matter and of only average fertility. They tolerate shade or sun well, seeming to prefer full sun in northern areas, and light shade in the hot South. However, their delicate colors tend to fade quickly in full sun. Too rich a soil leads to the rapid growth of lush foliage and few flowers. Space plants 18 to 36 inches apart.

Care is very easy. Water through dry periods and give an occasional light feeding. To improve appearance, remove the flower stalks after their blossoms are spent. The plant has no serious pests. Although some varieties can be left alone permanently, some of the more vigorous ones give improved performance with division every six or seven years. Division of mature plants is an arduous task due to the heavy root system, but it is still the best means of increase. Divide in spring or late summer.

Cultivars are too numerous to mention here. Extensive breeding has resulted in thousands.

HOSTA

For information on *Hosta,* see *Color in the Shade,* page 21.

Hydrangea macrophylla

Ilex verticullata

HYDRANGEA MACROPHYLLA

Bigleaf Hydrangea
Deciduous shrub
Dense shade to full sun
Hardy to Zone 7

This hydrangea, commonly grown in pots by florists, has an excellent late summer floral display (July to August) and lustrous, neat foliage in mild winter areas. Generally, however, varieties suitable as container plants are not as satisfactory in the garden. Outside, this hydrangea is a round shrub with many erect, infrequently branched stems reaching 4 to 8 feet in height (sometimes 12 feet) and spreading indefinitely, due to its tendency to sucker vigorously.

Many cultivars are available, and are generally divided between the *hortensias,* with all sterile flowers forming large globular heads, and the *lace-caps,* which have a delicate ring of large sterile flowers surrounding a cluster of tiny fertile ones. Flowers can be single or double; are available in white, pinks, and blues; and are generally clustered in heads that are 5 to 10 inches in diameter.

The bigleaf hydrangea prefers rather than just tolerates seashore conditions, where it can be planted in full sun. Otherwise, plant it in medium shade and in moist, rich, well-drained soil that is high in organic matter. In dense shade the plant will be leggy, and flowering will be reduced.

Soil acidity affects the uptake of aluminum by the plant, which in turn determines whether the flowers will be pink or blue. Blue flowers result from a pH of 5 to 5.5, while pink flowers occur in soils with a pH of 6 or higher. Apply aluminum sulfate to the soil to increase acidity and provide aluminum for blue flowers; apply lime to decrease the acidity for pink flowers. Either must be accomplished well before blooming to achieve the color desired. Bigleaf hydrangeas flower on old wood, so pruning should be done just after flowering. If the plant dies back from a hard winter, it will not produce flowers that season.

ILEX

Holly
Evergreen shrubs
Medium shade to full sun
Hardiness varies according to species

The hollies are highly ornamental trees or shrubs that are notable for their shiny green, leathery leaves and clusters of mostly red (sometimes yellow or black) berries. Some are self-fertile and others need both a male and a female plant to produce berries.

Hollies thrive in good, well-drained garden soil in medium shade to full sun. Regular watering is needed throughout the year. They can be pruned to shape and control growth. Holly leaf miner is their most serious insect pest. Spray with Orthene or diazinon when damage is first noticed. Mealybugs, white flies, and scale are occasional pests that are easily controlled.

Ilex cornuta (Chinese Holly; Hardy to Zone 7) is a large, upright shrub 10 to 15 feet tall; many smaller denser cultivars of this shrub are available as well. The leaves are an extremely handsome, dark, polished green in all seasons, and are larger and coarser than those of the Japanese holly. Profuse berries are normally a brilliant red.

Ilex crenata (Japanese Holly; Hardy to Zone 7) is commonly mistaken for boxwood because of its neat, rounded shape and dark green, dense, lustrous, fine-textured foliage. The berries of this species are black and inconspicuous. A slow-growing shrub that responds well to pruning, it will eventually reach 5 to 10 feet in height with a usually greater spread; older specimens may reach 20 feet or more.

Japanese holly is an excellent selection for hedges, foundation planting, and massing, and for an evergreen, soft texture in the shrub border. It transplants easily into moist, well-drained, slightly acid soils, does well in shade or sun, and is tolerant of pollution.

Ilex glabra (Inkberry; Hardy to Zone 3) is the hardiest broadleafed evergreen available to northern gardeners. The handsome, dark green foliage grows densely on younger plants in all seasons. Older plants often reach 6 to 8 feet in height by 8 to 10 feet in spread and develop a leggy openness, although this is quite variable. The berries are black and not particularly showy.

Ilex verticillata (Common Winterberry; Zones 4 to 8) is a deciduous holly that is unusual for its adaptability to wet, swampy soils, to which it is native. A popular plant in the eastern United States, it is an outstanding fruiting shrub that bears great quantities of bright red berries on bare branches far into the winter. Birds find the berries tasty, so the effective season often depends on their appetite. Winterberry can grow to 20 feet high in the wild, but usually reaches only 6 to 9 feet in the garden, with a similar spread. Be sure to plant a male within a few hundred feet of each female to ensure fruiting.

Ilex vomitoria (Yaupon; Hardy to Zone 8) is a small evergreen tree, although several cultivars are available, such as 'Nana' and 'Stokes', that are effectively dwarf (18 inches or less) and compact. Popular in the southeastern United States, this holly is more tolerant of alkaline soil and drought than other hollies. Its fine-textured foliage can easily be sheared into formal shapes. Although the species is considered one of the heaviest-fruiting of the hollies, the dwarf forms are generally sterile.

Iris kaempferi

Kalmia latifolia

For information on *Impatiens*, see *Color in the Shade*, page 20.

IRIS KAEMPFERI

Japanese Iris
Perennial
Light shade to full sun
Hardy to Zone 4

Massive, stately foliage and huge, flat blossoms distinguish this iris. It is quite finicky about location, but once established in moist, acid soil, it needs little attention for a long, colorful life.

The flowers are white, blue, purple, lavender, or pink. They are often 6 inches or more across. The three overlapping outer falls are large, flat, and held horizontally, and the inner standards are small and spreading. They bloom in late June and July. The dark green, swordlike leaves often grow 3 to 4 feet tall, and remain attractive all season. They are graceful, upright, and slightly arching in clusters topped by tall flowering stems. Stems usually grow 3 to 4 feet high, and heights of 6 feet are not uncommon in rich, boggy soil in mild climates. Japanese iris are restrained in growth and long-lived. Their rhizomes expand to form a clump.

The soil must be acid, very moist, and well supplied with organic matter. The plant tolerates and even thrives in boggy or frequently flooded areas. Lime and alkaline soil are usually fatal. Give them light shade or full sun. Space plants 18 to 24 inches apart.

Water iris abundantly and maintain acid soil conditions. Feed occasionally with acid plant food. This plant has no serious pests. Division is rarely needed for rejuvenation; most plants can be left undisturbed indefinitely. Division is an excellent means of increase, however, and is best performed in the spring, although it can be done in late summer after flowering.

Many hybrids are available in white, reddish purple, rose, lavender, blue, violet, purple, and various combinations thereof.

Iris pseudacorus (Water Flat Iris) is another large beardless iris that prefers very moist, acid conditions. The flowers are yellow and appear in great quantities atop 36 to 40-inch stems. This iris will self-sow prolifically in boggy, wet locations, and has become naturalized in many such areas in North America.

KALMIA LATIFOLIA

Mountain Laurel
Broad-leafed evergreen
Light shade
Zones 5 to 8

For spectacular white to deep pink flowers and excellent evergreen foliage, this eastern native is an undisputed treasure in any garden where it can be grown. Use it as a specimen and as a companion for azaleas and rhododendrons. Slow growing, in youth it is dense, rounded, and neat, becoming gnarled, picturesque, and open in old age. In the wild it can reach 30 to 35 feet high, but under cultivation 7 to 15 feet is a more usual figure. In the harsher climate of the Midwest, it rarely grows over a rounded 3 to 7 feet high.

Plant mountain laurel from a container into acid, cool, moist, well-drained soil that is high in organic matter. Light shade is appreciated, although full sun is tolerated. Mulch rather than cultivate around its shallow roots. This is not a good choice for dry, Mediterraneanlike climates or areas without frost (Zones 9 and 10). Cultivars are available for flower color from white to deep, bright pink.

KERRIA JAPONICA

Japanese Kerria
Deciduous shrub
Dense to light shade
Zones 5 to 8

This deciduous shrub has several appealing aspects. In winter, its thin, pistachio-green stems brighten the garden. If planted against a shaded wall or among more rampant plants, it can assume a graceful semivining habit, growing to 6 or 8 feet, and sometimes much higher. Its flowers appear in early spring and continue sporadically into summer in even the most shaded garden, although the plant may become sparse and leggy in dense shade. In autumn its leaves turn bright yellow. Kerria can be maintained at 2 to 3 feet in light shade, densely growing and suitable for the foreground of a shrub border. Kept low, it can help hide the dying foliage of bulbs. Its usual size, if unrestrained, is 4 to 6 feet tall and nearly as wide. Its most effective use is often not as an accent but as a softener of harsh lines, bare trunks, or walls.

Flowers of the species are single, golden-yellow, up to 2 inches wide. 'Pleniflora' (see below) produces golden yellow pompons 1½ inches in diameter. Flowers are borne singly and, in the spring, profusely. The leaves are up to 4 inches long, tapering, rich green on top and lighter underneath. They are pendulous on arching branches, contributing to an especially graceful effect.

Kerria is indifferent to soil and exposure, accepting deep shade, drought, and rather poor soil. Unless thinned, kerria can sucker heavily and become brambly. It is more attractive when kept open. Prune immediately after spring flowering, since it flowers on last year's wood. Fertilize only occasionally, and lightly. Richness encourages rampant growth.

K. j. 'aureo-variegata', seldom seen but worth looking for, is like the species except that it has yellow-edged leaves. *K. j.* 'picta'

Kerria japonica

Leucojum aestivum

Ligularia dentata

has white-edged leaves. *K. j.* 'plen-iflora', most common of the kerrias, has double flowers that last longer than the single flowers of the species.

LEUCOJUM

Leucojum
Bulb
Light shade to full sun
Hardy to Zone 6

Known as snowflakes, these are among the easiest bulbs to grow, and are especially attractive in a woodland setting.

Plant in light shade to full sun in the fall. No special care is necessary, and the bulbs flower best if left undisturbed for several years at a time. The fall snowflake does not fare well in warm climates.

Three species bloom at different times. The earliest is *L. vernum* (Spring Snowflake), with single bell flowers tipped in green on 6 to 9-inch stems. Slightly larger and bearing four to eight similar blossoms per stem is *L. aestivum* (Summer Snowflake). In early fall *L. autumnale* (Autumn Snowflake) puts in an appearance. There are usually two or three pinkish blossoms on each of the 4 to 6-inch stems. All snowflake bulbs send out several grassy leaves.

LEUCOTHOE FONTANESIANA

Drooping Leucothoe
Broad-leafed evergreen
Dense to medium shade
Zones 5 to 7

Most commonly planted in moist, acid, eastern gardens, the drooping leucothoe makes a terrific companion to rhododendrons, azaleas, and mountain laurel because of its dark, lustrous, evergreen foliage and graceful form. The bright green or bronze new foliage in the spring and the purplish winter color, along with the fragrant, delicate, white flowers in the spring, are important assets. Use leucothoe as a facer plant for leggy shrubs; as a graceful high ground cover for shady slopes; or for massing, grouping, or integrating into the shrub border. It is a perfect shrub to naturalize in a shady woodland wildflower garden.

L. fontanesiana transplants easily from a container in early spring, but is fastidious about its requirements. If given an acid, moist, well-drained soil that is high in organic matter, as well as dense to medium shade, ample moisture, and protection from drought and drying winds, it will prove to be a basically trouble-free plant, although leaf spot can be a problem. Pruning should be done directly after flowering, although it is seldom necessary due to the natural, graceful, fountainlike form of the plant, which grows 3 to 5 feet high and often wider. Older plants can be rejuvenated by pruning them clear to the ground.

'Girard's Rainbow' has yellow, green, and copper-variegated foliage. 'Nana' is a dwarf form that is 2 feet high and 6 feet wide.

LIGULARIA DENTATA

Golden Groundsel
Perennial
Light shade to full sun
Hardy to Zone 4

Large, bold leaves and tall spires of flowers make golden groundsel a useful specimen or border plant.

The small flowers are orange-yellow to bright yellow, about 2 inches across, and appear in large quantities held tightly against the tall flower stalks. They bloom in August. The deep green leaves have a purplish tint. They are broad, jagged, somewhat heart-shaped, and grow up to 12 inches across. They are effective all season, but are prone to droop and wilt in hot sun and during periods of high heat and high humidity.

The plant forms dense basal clumps of leaves up to 18 inches high. From these arise 30 to 40-inch stiffly vertical flower stalks. Clumps expand at a moderate rate through the growth of short rhizomes. The plant is fairly restrained in growth and is long-lived.

Golden groundsel needs moist, rich soil that is high in organic matter. Dry soil is quickly fatal, but the plant also resents sogginess. Light shade is best, although it tolerates full sun, especially in cool climates and moist soil. Hot sun causes unsightly drooping of the foliage, especially in humid weather. Space the plants 24 inches apart.

Care is moderately easy. Water abundantly and feed regularly. If necessary, bait for slugs and snails. Division, which is rarely necessary for maintenance, will be most successful if performed in the spring.

Ligustrum obtusifolium

Liriope muscari

Lobelia cardinalis

LIGUSTRUM

Privet
Evergreen and deciduous shrubs
Medium shade to full sun
Hardiness varies according to species

Pest-free, highly adaptable, and low in maintenance, the shrubby privets are most often used as formal and informal hedges, backgrounds, and screens. Most have white, spikey clusters of flowers in early summer, whose heavy scent is variously described as offensive to pleasant. All privets transplant easily bare root, are adaptable to nearly any soil except a wet one, and take medium shade to full sun. They perform well under adverse conditions of pollution and drought. If flowers are desired, prune just after blooming. Otherwise, prune any time. All privets grow rapidly and respond well to pruning and shaping.

Deciduous Types

Ligustrum amurense (Amur Privet; Hardy to Zone 4). A hardy privet that is excellent for hedges, it has good clean foliage, medium to fine in texture.

Ligustrum × ibolium (Ibolium Privet; Hardy to Zone 5). This shrub is similar to the California privet, but hardier.

Ligustrum obtusifolium (Border Privet; Hardy to Zone 4). In addition to being one of the hardiest privets, the border privet is also one of the most attractive because of its broad horizontal growth habit and dark green foliage. It will grow 10 to 12 feet tall and 12 to 15 feet wide, although it can easily be kept much smaller. Var. *regelianum* is a low, 4 to 5-foot-high shrub with unusual, horizontally spreading branches that are most attractive if allowed to grow naturally.

Ligustrum ovalifolium (California Privet; Hardy to Zone 6). Its glossy semievergreen leaves often tempt gardeners to grow this plant north of its range, where it dies to the ground every winter. Where hardy, it is a deservedly popular hedge plant.

Ligustrum × vicaryi (Golden Privet; Hardy to Zone 6). In full sun the leaves of this popular plant are a glaring yellow; in shade they are yellow-green to light green. Clipped hedges will remain yellow-green, since the shaded inner leaves are constantly exposed by clipping. 'Hillside Strain' is a hardier variety that is useful in Zone 5, although it is a gaudy plant, difficult to integrate into the landscape.

Ligustrum vulgare (Common Privet; Hardy to Zone 5). This is a plant to avoid because of its susceptibility to anthracnose. To lose mature hedge plants is an annoyance, to say the least.

Evergreen Types

Ligustrum japonicum (Japanese Privet; Hardy to Zone 7). Japanese privet makes an excellent hedge or screen in southern and western gardens. Because of its lustrous evergreen leaves, its dense, compact habit (it grows rapidly 6 to 12 feet high), and its responsiveness to pruning, this privet is also commonly used for training into topiary or small standards. An excellent container plant, it looks best when given plenty of water and protected from the hot sun. Many forms are available. This plant is frequently sold incorrectly to nurseries as *Ligustrum texanum*.

Ligustrum lucidum (Glossy Privet; Hardy to Zone 7). Often confused with the Japanese privet, this privet is more treelike, since it grows 35 to 40 feet high. To differentiate it from *L. japonicum* among young nursery plants, feel the undersides of the leaves. If the veins are raised, it is *L. japonicum*; if they are sunken, it is *L. lucidum*.

Ligustrum 'Suwanee River' is an evergreen hybrid that eventually grows 4 to 6 feet high, with a compact, tight habit. Its dark green, wavy leaves are useful as a low hedge or in a foundation planting.

LIRIOPE

Lilyturf
Ground cover
Medium shade to medium sun
Hardy to Zone 7

Liriope is characterized by clumps of coarse, mostly dark green, grasslike leaves up to 24 inches long and ¼ to ¾ inch wide. Like ophiopogon, with which it is sometimes confused, it is a member of the lily family. One difference between the two is that liriope is hardier. 'Big Blue' lilyturf (*L. muscari*) gets its name from its 4 to 8-inch-long, spikelike clusters of flowers that are, in fact, more violet than blue. They appear in good number among the leaves from about July into September and are followed by a few blue-black berries. This is the tallest of the lilyturfs, growing rather slowly to a height of 2 feet. It is sometimes listed as *Ophiopogon jaburan*.

Creeping lilyturf (*L. spicata*) is smaller in all aspects, forms a dense cover that spreads by underground stems, has pale lavender flowers, and grows at a moderate rate up to a foot high.

Lilyturf is excellent as a border along paths, under trees, in rock gardens, or as fill-in ground cover in small areas.

These plants have no special soil or light requirements, but are probably grown most often in medium to light shade, if only for reasons of landscape design. They need only light summer watering. Both are easily propagated by division. In extremely cold weather the leaves of both plants turn yellow and should be clipped off before new growth starts in spring. *L. spicata* is the hardiest, tolerating temperatures to -20°. *L. muscari* is damaged by temperatures below 0°.

LOBELIA CARDINALIS

Cardinal Flower
Perennial
Light shade to full sun
Hardy to Zone 2

The cardinal flower is a tall, stately plant with brilliant scarlet flowers in mid to late summer. It is a fine choice for moist, shady spots, especially in natural gardens.

The individual flowers are small and grow in a spike along the upper 6 or 8 inches of the stem. They bloom in late July to September, and are attractive to hummingbirds. The medium or dark green leaves are oblong or lance-shaped, growing to 4 inches long. They are arranged oppositely or in whorls along the stalks. The tall, vertical stems grow 3 to 4 feet high, and are topped with the blazing red flowers.

Mahonia aquifolium

Matteuccia pensylvanica

Unfortunately, the cardinal flower is short-lived. It will self-sow under optimum conditions, but this is not to be relied on. It is seldom, if ever, invasive.

Native to wet soils along streams and in boggy meadows and to woodland bottomlands, the cardinal flower does best in well-drained, sandy loam that is high in organic matter and kept evenly moist. Although tolerant of full sun if the soil is kept moist, it does best in light shade. It does not perform well in regions of mild winters. Space plants 12 to 18 inches apart.

Care is moderately difficult. Keep the plants well watered. Remove faded flower stalks. Mulch in the summer to retain moisture, and in winter to protect the crowns. Although several insects and fungal diseases may attack cardinal flowers, they are seldom serious enough to warrant protection. The plant should be divided annually to perpetuate it. Lift the clump, then remove and reset the outside clusters of new basal growth. This is best done in the early fall.

*MAHONIA AQUIFOLIUM
(BERBERIS AQUIFOLIUM)*

Oregon Grape, Oregon Grapeholly
Broad-leafed evergreen shrub
Medium to light shade
Zones 5 to 9

The Lewis and Clark expedition brought Oregon grape to the East Coast of the United States, where it has been popular ever since. This and related species are among the most adaptable and useful plants for the shade garden. They survive nearly anywhere, most of them in any soil and any degree of shade, and provide evergreen foliage and seasonal flowers and edible fruit. Oregon grape is not really a grape, but a member of the barberry family.

As an informal foundation planting, a specimen, or even a large-scale ground cover, Oregon grape is one of the most dependable shrubs. Its whorls of foliage grow on woody stems that can reach 6 to 8 feet but are usually lower. The height of the plant can be kept at 2 feet or less. Planted at 2-foot intervals, Oregon grape will form a tough, thick ground cover that chokes out even the most pernicious weeds. It creates an effective barrier, yet is graceful and delicate as a container plant. 'Compacta' stays at around 2 feet high, and spreads freely. It is bronze in winter.

The pinkish or bronzy new foliage of Oregon grape matures into leathery, spiny compound leaves up to 10 inches long, with 5 to 9 leaflets per leaf. In the Northwest they are cut and sold as Christmas greens.

The flowers are waxy and yellow, in clusters at the tips of branches, from March to May. Clusters of deep blue ¼-inch berries with a bloom succeed the flowers. These "grapes" were once marketed on the West Coast; they taste something like currants.

Oregon grape thrives virtually anywhere except in full sun of the hottest climates. Acid soil is best. It accepts summer water, as long as drainage is good, but tolerates long periods of drought. It should be pruned to maintain desired height. If attacked by the barberry looper, a defoliating caterpillar, spraying is necessary.

M. bealei (Leatherleaf Mahonia), native to China, grows in a strongly vertical habit from 6 to 12 feet high. Its fragrant yellow flowers in late winter and dense clusters of "grapes" are beautiful, but the most striking aspect of the plant is its symmetrical, horizontally-held compound leaves—up to 15 inches long, dark blue-green, and spiny. It strongly prefers rich soil and moisture; medium to light shade is necessary.

M. lomariifolia (Burmese Mahonia) has leaves to 24 inches long and 6 inches wide. Flowers are similar to those of *M. aquifolium* and *M. bealei*. It grows to 12 feet high and, unlike *M. bealei*, branches with age. It too likes rich, moist soil and medium to light shade. If you want a bold, tropical effect in a shaded entryway and your climate area doesn't allow tree ferns or other tropicals, perhaps this or *M. bealei* is the solution. It lends itself to container culture. It is less hardy than other species; hardy to Zone 7.

M. nervosa (Longleaf Mahonia) has 10 to 20-inch leaves, erect stems 2 feet or taller, and a more polished appearance than *M. aquifolium*. This native of northwestern North America woodlands spreads to make an excellent ground cover with neat 12 to 18-inch glossy green leaves. It does best in rich, moist soil and light to medium shade.

M. pinnata (California Holly Grape) closely resembles *M. aquifolium* except that its leaves are spinier and more crinkly. It does best in light shade. Native to southern and central California, it is particularly tolerant of poor soil, drought, and heat—a tough plant that makes an excellent barrier.

M. repens (Creeping Mahonia), a 10-inch-tall bluish green ground cover from the American Northwest, stays uniformly low and spreads quickly to form a dense mat over medium or small areas, including slopes, in any degree of shade. Except in scale, it closely resembles *M. aquifolium*.

*MATTEUCCIA
PENSYLVANICA*

Ostrich Fern
Fern
Deep shade to medium sun
Hardy to Zone 2

The ostrich fern is one of the largest ferns native to central and northern North America. Under optimum growing conditions, the fronds grow at least 4 to 6 feet tall, and sometimes taller. The fronds are a lustrous dark green and grow from a central crown. Underground runners rapidly grow outward from the crown and spread easily into nearby areas. This fern should be planted only in large areas where it can grow freely. The fronds are deciduous and turn brown with the first fall frost. The bronze, fertile fronds stand erect over the winter. The ostrich fern is native to marshes, swamps, and shallow creeks. It grows best in a sandy, slightly acid (pH 5.5 to 6.5) soil that is high in organic matter. Keep the soil moist. This fern thrives in areas with light shade, but can tolerate alternate sunlight if the soil is kept moist. The ostrich fern is easy to grow, but because of its height, it is most effectively used as a background plant. Plants should be set 3 feet apart to allow room for spreading.

Mentha requienii

Mimulus species

Mertensia virginica

Myosotis sylvatica

Corsican Mint
Ground cover
Light shade to full sun
Hardy to Zone 7

M. requienii (Corsican mint) is the lowest-growing of the many species and dozens of cultivars of mint. It spreads rapidly by underground stems, forming a soft green carpet 1 to 3 inches high. Tiny oval leaves, about ⅛ inch across, grow opposite on slender stems and give off a strong minty fragrance when bruised. Tiny lavender-colored flowers appear in midsummer.

Corsican mint grows equally well in light shade or sun. In a well-drained fairly rich soil kept on the moist side, it is a vigorous grower. It is easily propagated by division; set new plants 6 inches apart. It also self-sows.

MERTENSIA VIRGINICA

Virginia Bluebells
Perennial
Dense to light shade
Hardy to Zone 3

The Virginia bluebells have drooping, bell-shaped flowers that appear in the spring. The erect, leafy plants are most attractive in an informal or wild garden.

The outer portion of the petals is sky blue and the inner part pinkish or purplish. Each flower is about an inch long, and they are produced in clusters that hang gracefully at the ends of branching stems. They bloom in April and May. All foliage dies back and usually has disappeared by July. Virginia bluebell is restrained in growth and not invasive, but will self-sow here and there.

The plant prefers a cool, moist soil high in organic matter, and is partial to dense shade. It does best in the cool-summer climates of the northern latitudes. Space plants 8 to 12 inches apart.

Mulching will help keep soil cool and moist in the summer and also provide a continual supply of decaying organic matter. Keep the soil evenly moist but never soggy. Do not remove the foliage when it starts to degenerate, but allow it to die down naturally, as with bulbs.

MIMULUS

Monkey Flower
Annuals and perennials
Dense to light shade
Hardiness varies according to species

Mimulus is a genus of moisture-loving annuals and perennials that thrive in some degree of shade. They are not to be confused with the related *Diplacus* species, a dry-growing and sun-loving species also called monkey flower and often included in the genus *Mimulus*. All species have bright-colored tubular flowers and repeat bloom if cut back after the first flowering. Otherwise, species and their cultural requirements are so varied that they are discussed individually below. These are the most widely available.

M. cardinalis (Scarlet Monkey Flower), a perennial native to the western United States, produces slender 2-inch scarlet flowers with two lips, from midsummer into autumn. Heavily branched and loose-growing to 2½ feet tall, it requires light shade and constant moisture. In its native habitat it often grows in seeps and shallow streams. Beds, borders, and bogs are suitable settings. Kept wet, it withstands extreme heat. Hardy to Zone 7.

M. cupreus (*M. hybridus*), native to Chile, is an annual that grows 6 to 12 inches tall in bogs. Not important in itself as a garden subject, it is the parent of many popular large-flowered hybrid annuals. Among them are 'Bees' Dazzler' (scarlet), 'Leopard' (yellow with red or orange spots), 'Plumtree' (pink), 'Queen's Prize' (yellow and pink), 'Red Emperor' (scarlet), and 'Whitecroft Scarlet' (vermillion). The Monarch strain has especially large flowers. Hybrids, 6 to 8 inches high, start easily from seed cast on the surface of damp soil. Useful in planters, in beds and borders, along streams, or beside garden pools, they adapt easily to boggy conditions. Medium shade is best, but both light and dense shade are possible. All like rich soil, a cool location, and regular fertilizing.

M. lewisii, a British Columbian perennial often grown as an annual, is quite similar to *M. cardinalis* in culture and appearance, except that it has pink flowers beautifully spotted with maroon and lined with yellow. Variety 'Albus' has white flowers. *M. lewisii* likes light shade and moisture with drainage. Hardy to Zone 7.

M. luteus (Monkey Musk), a wet-growing Chilean perennial, grows about a foot high and reseeds freely in boggy areas. The 2-inch-wide flowers are yellow, spotted with red or purple. Hardy to Zone 7.

MYOSOTIS SYLVATICA

Forget-me-not
Biennial often treated as an annual
Medium shade to full sun

In late summer or early fall, after planting a bed of bulbs, cast about a generous supply of forget-me-not seeds. You will be rewarded in spring with a beautiful blue haze as the perfect backdrop for

Nandina domestica

Nicotiana alata

Niermbergia hippomanica

daffodils and tulips, one that will keep the bed colorful well into early summer.

Forget-me-nots reseed abundantly to perform year after year. Its tiny blue, pink, or white flowers bloom generously on delicate, multibranched stems 6 to 12 inches tall.

Forget-me-nots prefer fertile, moist, well-drained soil that is rich in organic matter, and perform well in wet soil. They prefer light shade, but will tolerate full sun. Water and feed them liberally. They do best in regions with long, cool springs. Elsewhere, spring crops will set seeds and die out. Then, after late-summer rains, a second crop will come up to give you fall color.

Nandina; Heavenly Bamboo
Broad-leafed evergreen shrub (semideciduous in the North)
Medium shade to full sun
Hardy to Zone 7

Not even remotely related to true bamboo, nandina is a popular shrub in southern gardens for its variety of ornamental assets and easy care. Its strongly vertical form contrasts nicely with delicate, wispy foliage that is evergreen in mild climates. Erect, creamy white flower spikes borne on the ends of the vertical branches in June are followed by bright red clusters of berries.

With a few hours of sun a day, nandina frequently has brilliant crimson to purple foliage in the fall and winter. Often reaching 8

feet in height and 2½ to 3 feet in width, nandina is effective as a hedge or screen, in a mass or grouping, or as a solitary specimen in an entryway or container. It is particularly effective when backlit. Nandina will lose its leaves at 10°F, and will die back to the ground at 0°F, although it quickly recovers the following season. In the northern limits of its range, it is best used as an herbaceous perennial.

Since crossfertilization improves fruiting, try to plant nandina in groups. It performs well in nearly any soil, in medium shade to full sun, although some protection is required in particularly hot climates. Established plants tolerate drought well. Prune out old, leggy canes annually to encourage density. Nandina competes well with tree roots, and is little troubled by pests, although it will exhibit chlorosis in alkaline soils.

Several cultivars are offered for form, dwarf size, foliage color, and improved hardiness.

Flowering Tobacco, Nicotiana
Annual
Medium shade to full sun

Nicotiana reaches the height of grace when massed in large beds. Each plant is anchored by a low rosette of large leaves from which spring tall, slender stems. Long, thin tubes at right angles to the stem open into star-shaped flowers in white and shades of mauve, red, maroon, pink, yellow, green, and yellow-green. The nodding, delicate effect is enhanced by planting in great masses, especially in areas with a gentle wind.

Often touted as powerfully fragrant, the day-blooming hybrids available today are sorely disappointing. Occasionally a fresh, sweet scent can be detected in the vicinity of a bed, especially on cool evenings; but the famous perfume, sadly, has been lost. It can be found only in the tall, old-fashioned, evening-blooming kinds.

Consider nicotiana when looking for a tall (12 to 36 inches), delicate statement in the mixed border. It is surprisingly effective planted in clumps in large pots. Do not grow nicotiana near where you intend to grow tomatoes; it attracts many pests and diseases that may attack tomatoes, such as tobacco mosaic virus. While the hardy nicotiana will be little troubled, the tomatoes may not survive.

Nicotiana is gaining favor as an alternative to petunias in areas where the humidity-related disease botrytis can snip the blossoms off for several weeks in late summer.

It does best in fertile, well-drained, moist soil that is high in organic matter. Medium to light shade is preferred, but it will tolerate full sun in humid climates; flowers will fade some in full sun in dry climates. Fertilize regularly, and keep the soil moist. It will self-sow freely, but is not difficult to control.

Cup Flower
Tender perennial grown as an annual
Light shade to full sun

Although little-known and usually hard to find, the cup flower is a diminutive delight in the garden. Neat, spreading mounds of the fine-textured foliage are smothered with blue-violet or purple flowers all summer long. Flowers hold their color without fading even in the brightest sun.

Nierembergia is outstanding in large beds or as a 6 to 12-inch ground cover, but is even more elegant and appropriate grown in small patches in the rock garden. It behaves well as an edging to a border or walkway, and can be planted in pots, hanging baskets, and window boxes. It is also a logical substitute for trailing lobelia where the latter dies out in the heat.

For its easy care, long-season blue-violet color, and restrained size, the cup flower deserves greater popularity.

It needs fertile, sandy, moist, well-drained soil that is high in organic matter, and light shade to full sun. Shade is preferred in areas with hot summers. Keep the plants moist, but be careful not to overwater.

Ophiopogon japonicus

OPHIOPOGON JAPONICUS

Mondograss
Ground cover
Medium to light shade
Hardy to Zone 7

Mondograss (*O. japonicus*) is the most grasslike of the lilyturfs. It is identified by dense clumps of long, ⅛-inch-wide leaves that arch over into mounds 8 to 10 inches high. The leaves are dark green and coarse in texture. Small, pale purple flowers, mostly hidden among the leaves, appear in July and August, followed by pea-sized blue fruit. Mondograss spreads by means of fleshy subsurface stems. The growth rate is quite slow until the plant is well established.

A miniature version of *O. japonicus*, growing about half as high, is *O.j.* 'Nana'. *O. jaburan* is similar in size and growth habit to *Liriope muscari*, and is often mistaken for it. The chief observable differences are that *O. jaburan* has green instead of brownish stems, and white, more drooping, less tightly clustered flowers. *O.* 'Variegatus' is a low-growing variety with white, striated leaves.

These plants are adaptable to most well-drained soils. In coastal areas they will grow in full sun; elsewhere they look and grow best in medium to light shade. All need regular summer watering. Mondograss needs more frequent watering if exposed to full sun

Osmunda cinnamomea

in a mass planting. New plants can be started by dividing clumps. Set divisions of mondograss 6 inches apart, *O. jaburan* 12 inches apart.

Mondograss looks good as a sizable planting under the shade of a large tree. In a shaded patio setting, a few dozen plants, placed about 8 inches apart with baby's-tears (*Soleirolia soleirolii*) in between, produce a lovely, cool effect. It also makes a handsome border along paths, and is useful in defining and separating lawns from flower beds. *O. jaburan* is most effective where its attractive flowers (good for cutting) and violet-blue fruits can be seen close up, as in entryways, near fences and buildings, and under trees.

OSMANTHUS FRAGRANS

Sweet Olive
Broad-leafed evergreen shrub
Medium to light shade
Hardy to Zone 8

While its powerfully fragrant, nearly year-round flowers are an attraction, sweet olive is also a compact, neat plant with glossy evergreen foliage that makes an outstanding hedge, screen, background, espalier, or container plant. It is very easy to care for and quite adaptable. Plant sweet olive in any soil, from sand to clay, give it medium to light shade, and it will grow at a moderate rate to a 10-foot-wide and -high shrub with a rounded outline. It can easily be kept lower, however, and responds well to shearing. Prune any time of year; pinch the growing tips to encourage denseness.

'Aurianticus' has powerfully fragrant orange blossoms that concentrate their bloom in October.

Osmanthus heterophyllus (Holly Olive; Hardy to Zone 7) is perhaps the handsomest of the *Osmanthus* species. It is often confused with English holy. Holly has alternate leaves, while *Osmanthus* always has opposite leaves. Holly olive has lustrous, spiny, dark green leaves and fragrant, hidden, yellow flowers in the fall. It is unusually shade tolerant. A number of cultivars are available with variegated foliage.

Pachysandra terminalis

Osmanthus delavayi (Delavay Osmanthus; Hardy to Zone 8) is distinguished by its small, fine-textured leaves and a graceful, arching habit, along with the largest white flowers of the genus. They are profuse and fragrant from late March to May. Particularly handsome on banks and walls where branches can cascade, it also responds well to pruning as a hedge or foundation plant.

OSMUNDA CINNAMOMEA

Cinnamon Fern
Fern
Deep shade to medium sun
Hardy to Zone 4

Native to boggy areas of the eastern United States and Canada, the cinnamon fern is one of the earliest ferns to emerge in the spring. Young fronds are covered with white, woolly hair before they unfurl. When full grown, the waxy fronds are yellow-green and grow 24 to 36 inches tall and 6 to 8 inches wide. There are two distinctly different types of fronds—fertile and sterile. The fertile frond resembles a cinnamon stick. It emerges first, and after releasing its spores it turns golden brown, withers, and lies on the ground through the summer. The sterile fronds appear in late spring, stay green all summer, and turn brown with the first fall frost. This fern requires a slightly acid (pH 5.5 to 6.5) soil that is kept evenly moist. It spreads slowly, and because of its height, it is best used as a background plant.

Pieres japonica

Pittosporum tobira

Pachysandra, Japanese Spurge
Ground cover
Dense to light shade
Hardy to Zone 4

Pachysandra is reportedly the most popular shade ground cover in the United States. This is not surprising, because it has a lot going for it: it is evergreen; hardy; lush; fast-covering; perfect for large or small areas, medium or dense shade; indifferent to tree roots; attractively flowering; and long-lived. It spreads by branching underground runners. In dense shade it grows to almost a foot high; in light to medium shade, 6 to 8 inches.

Pachysandra produces small fluffy spikes of greenish white flowers in the spring. Established plants occasionally produce whitish berries in the fall. Four-inch-long leaves, growing in whorls at the tops of stems, make a dense, even cover.

Pachysandra prefers moist, acid, well-drained soil, but will accept somewhat compacted, root-matted soil. Because its runners are rather invasive, it should be planted only where it is contained or where its spreading will do no harm to the design of the garden or to less vigorous plants. It can compete all too successfully with broad-leafed evergreens for food and moisture, but will not tolerate foot traffic.

Spring feeding with a complete fertilizer is helpful. Tree leaves disappear into it and should be left alone, as they form a beneficial mulch. If planting becomes open, cut back lightly to encourage denser growth.

'Green Carpet' is hardier, more compact, and denser than the species. It is darker green, and flowers more heavily. 'Silveredge' has lighter green leaves with a silvery white margin of ¼ inch or less.

P. procumbens (Allegheny Spurge), native to the Appalachians, is clumping and erect, to a foot high. In colder regions it is deciduous. Its white or pinkish fragrant spring flowers are especially attractive.

Japanese Pieris, Japanese Andromeda
Broad-leafed evergreen shrub
Medium to light shade
Zones 6 to 9

This refined cousin of the rhododendron and azalea mixes beautifully with its relatives and various acid growers such as ferns and other woodland plants. A neat evergreen shrub with a compact habit, pieris requires no pruning. It grows slowly to 6 to 12 feet high and 6 to 8 feet wide, with a slightly drooping habit. Its delicate sprays of buds, white or pink flowers, seed capsules, attractive deep green mature foliage, and brilliantly-colored bronzy red new foliage in spring make it singularly beautiful throughout the year. As a specimen, part of a shrub border, a mass planting, or a container subject, it is a classic for medium to light shade. Several cultivars are available, including a variegated compact form with white-edged leaves.

Buds appear in autumn, and develop in late winter or early spring into gracefully pendulous 6-inch clusters of white or pinkish bell-shaped blossoms resembling lily-of-the-valley—hence one of its common names, lily-of-the-valley shrub. The flowers are long-lasting.

Thin, oblong leaves, to 3 inches long and an inch wide, are pink to bronzy red as they emerge in spring. They mature to glossy, deep green, creating a tiered effect.

In most climates light shade is good, but particularly in very hot climates, medium shade is best. Pieris should be sheltered from the wind and winter sun in cold areas. Soil should be rich, high in organic content, acid, and fast-draining. If pruning is ever necessary—and it never is, except to shape the plant—prune immediately after flowering. Crown rot, fungus leaf spot, a dieback fungus, lace bugs, scales, and mites can be severe problems unless controlled by appropriate sprays.

P. floribunda (Mountain Pieris, Mountain Andromeda; Zones 5 to 8), native to the eastern United States, is quite similar to *P. japonica* in appearance and requirements but more compact and smaller (2 to 6 feet high and wide), and it flowers in April. Flowers are pure white. A very old specimen in an English garden is 6 feet high and 15 feet wide. *P. floribunda* is less vulnerable to pests than is *P. japonica*.

P. 'Forest Flame', a 6 to 7-foot hybrid between *P. japonica* and *P. forestii,* has vivid scarlet new growth and is hardier than *P. forestii.*

P. forestii (Chinese Pieris) is more tender than other species. It closely resembles them but is denser and larger, and its new growth is more brilliantly colored. Hardy to Zone 8.

Tobira, Japanese Pittosporum
Broad-leafed evergreen shrub
Dense shade to full sun
Zones 8 to 10

Dark green, leathery, evergreen foliage; fragrant, early, creamy yellow spring flowers with a scent like orange blossoms; and a broad, dense habit all have made this a popular plant in southern and western gardens for screens, massed plantings, borders, and as foundation plantings. It is particularly effective in containers or trained as a small, crooked-stemmed tree.

Smaller cultivars, some of which have variegated foliage, are available for facing plants and ground covers. However, another selection is suggested if a formal hedge is desired—this pittosporum does not respond well to hard pruning or shearing, although frequent light pinching can help to maintain a compact habit. Allowed to grow naturally, it reaches 6 to 15 feet in height and is usually slightly wider. Fairly drought-resistant, it nevertheless appreciates adequate water and an annual light fertilization. Aphids and scale can be a problem. Medium shade to full sun is best, although it tolerates dense shade well.

Polygonatum odoratum
'Variegatum'

Polypodium species

Polystichum mumitum

POLYGONATUM
COMMUTATUM

Great Solomon's Seal
Perennial
Dense to light shade
Hardy to Zone 4

This subtle woodland native has long, attractive, arching stems and hanging clusters of tiny flowers. It is one of those rare plants that will thrive in dry shade.

The flowers are yellowish green to greenish white, about ½ inch long, bellshaped, and droop in small clusters all along the undersides of the stems. They bloom in May and early June. Foliage is the chief attraction of this plant. The rich green to bluish green leaves grow up to 7 inches long. They are held perpendicular to the stem, and alternate along its length.

Great Solomon's seal is best grown in cool, moist soil well amended with organic matter. However, it will tolerate dry soil and intensive root competition quite well. Give it dense to light shade. Space plants 18 to 36 inches apart.

Water adequately and mulch over the summer. This plant has no serious pests. Although never required for rejuvenation, division for increase is easy when performed in early spring.

POLYPODIUM VULGARE

Common Polypody
Fern
Light shade to light sun
Hardy to Zone 4

The common polypody creeps over rocks and boulders and is sometimes called the rock-cap fern. It is native to north and central North America. The yellow-green, leathery fronds grow 10 inches long and 2 inches wide. They are evergreen, even in severe winters, and curl up and turn dark green as the temperatures drop. These fronds remain on the plant long after new fronds emerge in the spring. The fronds leave a scar on the rhizome when they break off. The rhizomes form a dense mat that is partially exposed above the soil surface. This fern grows best in a loamy-woodland type of soil. It tolerates short periods of dry soil, but regular watering improves the appearance. It prefers light shade, but if the soil is kept constantly moist, alternate sunlight is satisfactory. This fern is most ideally planted in crevices between rocks, where the rhizomes are allowed to creep in their characteristic manner.

POLYSTICHUM

Shield Fern
Fern
Dense shade
Hardy to Zone 4

Polystichum species is a large group of ferns, including many natives of North American forests. They are hardy and usually evergreen, with sword-shaped fronds, and are similar to wood ferns (dryopteris). However, the rough, sawtoothed edges of the shield fern fronds are a distinguishing characteristic. Shady woodlands and rock gardens are the most common places for these plants.

The Christmas fern (*P. acrostichoides*) is native from Nova Scotia to Florida. The common name is due to the commercial availability of its fronds for use in Christmas decorations. It is also used as a house plant.

The western sword fern (*P. munitum*) is native to a range extending from Alaska, south to California, and east to Montana. Its fronds are leathery, 2 to 3½ feet long, and up to 10 inches wide at the base.

Moisture, dense shade, and a humus-rich soil are the most important needs of these ferns. Propagate by dividing the underground runners in the spring.

PRATIA ANGULATA

Pratia
Ground cover
Medium shade to full sun
Hardy to Zone 7

English gardeners with their keen eyes for the beautiful and useful began growing pratia in the last century, but it is still a sleeper in the United States. This lushest of low ground covers is attractive year-round, with its evergreen foliage, liberal sprinkling of lobelialike flowers through summer and autumn, and pea-size violet to purple berries.

In sun or very light shade, with proper feeding and watering, it forms a tight carpet to 5 inches tall that usually keeps out weeds and grasses. In medium shade, its habit is looser and taller, to a foot high. Particularly valuable to West Coast gardeners who want a bright green ground cover for areas beneath oaks, pratia can grow—but only in the shade—in dry soil with an occasional light sprinkling once it is established there. Autumn planting assures that it will get established during the rainy season. Its appropriateness for the rock garden should not be overlooked. Wherever it is planted, it will spread rapidly by rooting stems if the soil is moist.

The flowers, ½ to ¾ inch wide, are white and strikingly similar to those of the related *Lobelia erinus*. The leaves, ¾ inch long with slightly serrated edges, are rich, lustrous green, and, like the stems, rather succulent.

In hotter areas pratia must have at least light shade. Soil must drain fast. High sand content is desirable but not mandatory. Plugs spaced at 6 to 12-inch intervals cover rapidly.

In bright, warm spots moisture is necessary and richness is desirable. Occasional feeding with mild fertilizer such as fish emulsion benefits pratia grown in such spots. Pratia grown in medium shade prefers a more austere regimen—not only less watering, but less feeding. It will not withstand foot traffic.

PRIMULA

For information on *Primula*, see *Color in the Shade*, page 24.

PULMONARIA SACCHARATA

Bethlehem Sage
Ground cover
Dense to light shade
Hardy to Zone 4

Bethlehem sage's deep green leaves speckled with white make an attractive ground cover in the shade. Small flowers in early spring are a decided extra advantage, and it is easy to grow.

The flowers come in blue, reddish violet, or white. Individually they are trumpetlike and

Pulmonaria saccharata
'Mrs. Moon' *with hostas*

Sagina subulata

Salvia splendens

about ½ inch long. They appear in relaxed clusters on stalks 10 to 12 inches tall. The flowers are often pink in bud, changing to blue as they open. They bloom in early April and May. The attractive, glossy leaves are oval to heart-shaped, and grow to about 6 inches long. The basal rosettes of leaves reach 6 to 8 inches in height. From each crown arise several flowering stalks. The foliage remains attractive all season.

The crowns gradually expand by producing more leaves at the outer edge of the clump. The plant is long-lived, restrained in growth, and not invasive.

Bethlehem sage prefers moist soil that is high in organic matter, although it need not be fertile. Give these plants partial to deep shade, and space them 10 inches apart. They require little attention. Watering is beneficial during dry spells. They have no serious pests. Although it is seldom required, division is an excellent means of increase. It is best done in late summer or very early spring, although success is common even during full bloom. Water heavily after transplanting.

Pulmonaria saccharata 'Mrs. Moon' is a form with larger flowers that are pink in bud and bright blue when open.

P. angustifolia (Blue Lungwort) has plain dark green leaves that are quite hairy, almost bristly. The flowers are showy, pink in bud, opening to blue, and appear in April and May. Several varieties are available, including pink, salmon, white, and red ones. These may be listed as *P. saccharata* in some sources.

REHMANNIA ELATA

Rehmannia
Perennial
Light shade
Hardy to Zone 9

It is curious that this spectacular perennial is so little known in the gardens of the more moderate climate zones. Its blossoms are no less beautiful than those of its cousin the foxglove, to which it bears a clear family resemblance. From spring to late autumn, an established clump blooms continuously on thin 2 to 4-foot spikes. As it becomes established, what began as a modest plant becomes a sizable clump spreading by underground stems. Where there is little frost it is evergreen. In borders and planters its slim spikes of sparse but showy flowers create casual beauty. They are useful in arrangements.

The dusky rose-pink flowers, to 3 inches long, are tubular with widely flaring lips. Yellowish or golden throats are heavily speckled with deep red. Like typical foxglove flowers, these are rather pendulous on the spikes. Deeply cut, irregular leaves, to 8 inches long, are concentrated beneath the spikes. Leaves on the spikes are toward the base, and small.

Rehmannia prefers light shade. In denser shade it holds its own but blooms sparsely on spindly stems, and clumps enlarge slowly. Moist soil rich in organic matter is best. Occasional feeding with high-phosphorus fertilizer during the long blooming season is beneficial. In cold areas, cover with mulch as it goes dormant.

'Alba', a creamy-white variety, is occasionally sold.

RHODODENDRON

For information on *Rhododendron*, see *Color in the Shade*, pages 14–17.

SAGINA SUBULATA

Irish Moss and Scotch Moss
Ground cover
Light shade
Hardy to Zone 5

Dark green *Sagina subulata* (Irish Moss) and its golden green form, *S. s.* 'Aurea' (Scotch Moss) have a pair of look-alikes that wrongly bear the same common names and are used similarly in the garden: *Arenaria verna* and *A. v.* 'Aurea'. The more common genus is *Sagina*. Neither genus is a true moss. *Sagina* is a relative of dianthus, and a close look at the tiny white flowers sprinkled over it in the summer and the tiny, awl-like leaves reveal a family resemblance. Scotch and Irish moss are useful in lightly shaded gardens as a fine-textured evergreen ground cover or lawn substitute for small areas, as filler between stepping stones, and as an accent among rocks. They form a soft, mossy carpet 1 to 4 inches high.

Light shade and rich, moist, well-drained soil are best. Occasional foot traffic is not very damaging. In mild-summer areas Irish and Scotch moss accept medium to full sun. Plant plugs 6 to 8 inches apart. They spread quickly, and humps can be leveled somewhat by pressing gently with your foot. Occasional fertilizing with a mild liquid fertilizer keeps them looking their best. They require constant moisture but not wetness.

SALVIA SPLENDENS

Scarlet Sage
Annuals
Light shade to full sun

It's no wonder that scarlet sage is one of the most popular spike-flowered annuals for large-scale bedding and bright color, especially in parks and other public places. It requires little attention and provides some of the brightest, most intense annual reds and scarlets known to the gardener. It also comes in pastel shades of pink, mauve, and white. And yet, in spite of its popularity, its versatility has been largely unexploited. *Salvia,* which grows 6 to 36 inches in height, is excellent to provide splashes of accent among other annuals in an informal border. It performs beautifully in light shade, although flowering a bit later. Another delightful attribute is that hummingbirds love them. If for no other reason, this makes *Salvia splendens* a delight for pots and patios. It holds up well in intense heat, and is long-lasting when cut.

Salvia prefers well-drained, moist, rich soil that is high in organic matter. Although it grows well in full sun, partial shade is best for varieties with pastel or cream colors, which fade in full sun. Keep well watered, although it is tolerant of mild drought. Fertilize monthly.

Scilla hispanica

Senecio × hybridus

Fragrant Sarcococca
Evergreen shrub
Dense to light shade
Hardy to Zone 7

Fragrant sarcococca is as undemanding and reliable as any shrub in the garden. Even in dense shade, and in the drabness of winter and early spring, it provides evergreen foliage, fragrant flowers, and bright, showy berries. Properly situated, it can endure neglect quite happily. Its slow growth rate and drought tolerance make it easy to maintain. Sarcococca grows 3 to 6 feet high and spreads as wide. It is especially valuable in dark entryways, beneath low trees, espaliered, or around the shade garden as a high ground cover.

Small white flowers appear in late winter or early spring, nearly hidden by foliage but very noticeably fragrant. Even as it blooms, the plant retains the fleshy ¼-inch scarlet berries produced the year before. The waxy, deep green, wavy-edged leaves, to 2 inches long and ½ inch wide, are consistently attractive throughout the year.

Any degree of shade is acceptable. Acid, rich soil is best, but almost any well-drained soil will do. The only pest to watch for is scale.

S. hookeriana humilis (S. humilis) can reach 4 feet high but seldom exceeds 1½ feet. A more vigorous spreader than *S. ruscifolia*, it can spread several feet slowly by underground stems. For a quick ground cover, space plants 9 to 12 inches apart. Berries are blue-black. Otherwise it is quite similar in appearance, and in requirements, to *S. ruscifolia*.

Bluebells
Bulb
Light shade to full sun

Not all bluebells are blue; some are purple, violet, pink, rose, or white. But all the following members of the *Scilla* genus produce bell-shaped blossoms borne in clusters on leafless stalks. Some produce as many as 100 blooms per stalk; others, no more than a few. Basal leaves of the plants are strap-shaped. Although nothing is as beautiful as a woodland garden sprinkled with bluebells, they are also attractive in pots.

Scilla bifolia (Two-Leafed Squill) is the earliest-blooming bluebell. Blooms resemble open bells or stars in turquoise, white, violet, or purplish pink. Up to 8 flowers about 1 inch across are carried on stems that grow to 8 inches.

The Spanish bluebell, *S. hispanica* (sometimes still listed as S. campanulata), is the most popular species of the genus. Its 15 to 20-inch stems carry about 12 nodding bells each half an inch across. Varieties are available in white and pink, as well as in blue.

The English bluebell, *S. nonscripta* (or *S. nutans*), is also known as the wood hyacinth. Its bells are smaller than those of the Spanish bluebell, and the stalks grow to only 12 inches. It forms a carpet of blue in spring, or you may choose white or pink variations.

In spite of their name, Peruvian bluebells or squills are native to the Mediterranean region. *S. peruviana* flowers are bluish purple and borne in a dramatic, dome-shaped cluster instead of the gentle, elongated clusters of the other scillas. Stalks are 10 to 12 inches high. A single plant in a large pot makes a striking patio accent.

S. tubergeniana blooms in late winter or early spring. It produces only one to four flowers clustered along 5-inch stalks, but each bulb sends up several stalks.

Cold-weather gardeners take special delight in Siberian squill, or *S. siberica*, with its dainty, flaring, intense-blue bells on 3 to 6-inch stems. This is one of the best for naturalizing, especially under deciduous trees.

Cut scillas for the house when half the spike has opened its flowers. They will last for up to a week.

Plant scillas in the fall in sun or light shade. All species need plenty of moisture during the growing season. They also prefer being left alone for several years. Don't overlook scillas when composing your indoor garden. They make lovely houseplants.

Cineraria
Annual
Medium to dense shade

Cinerarias are easy-to-grow, shade-loving plants. Their daisy-like flowers are 2 to 4 inches across and bloom in a wide range of colors, including blue, pink, red, purple, lavender, and white. The oval, bright green leaves and slightly woolly stems set off the bright velvet flowers. The plants grow 18 inches tall and can be grown directly in the ground among shrubs, in beds, and as border plants. They also grow well in containers and window boxes for brightening patios and porches. For best growth, keep the plants slightly pot bound. Cinerarias are grown as annuals in all but the warmest areas of the country. They are native to the Canary Islands, and thrive in deep to light shade.

Cinerarias grow easily from seed if they are sprouted and grown in a cool (45° to 55°F) area. Start them indoors from late spring to early fall for bloom the following spring and summer. If you don't have cool growing conditions with plenty of light, purchase the plants from a nursery or florist. Plant them 10 to 12 inches apart. Cinerarias prefer a well-drained soil that is high in organic matter content. Plants wilt easily as the soil dries, so keep the soil evenly moist with regular waterings.

Soleirolia (Helxine soleirolii)

Taxus baccata

Torenia fournieri

SOLEIROLIA

Baby's-tears
Ground cover
Dense to light shade
Zone 10

Baby's-tears *(S. soleirolii, Helxine soleirolii)* is a creeping, mosslike plant that forms a dense, soft carpet 1 to 3 inches high. The foliage is composed of tiny, light green, rounded leaves growing in a tight mat.

This is a plant for shade, rich soil, and moisture. It is quickly killed by too much direct sun, drought, or subfreezing temperature. Propagate by division, planting sections 6 to 12 inches apart. A variant having golden yellow foliage is available in some nurseries. For outdoor use only in warmest regions.

Baby's-tears provides a cool, delicate effect planted at the base of trees or shade plants like ferns, camellias, and azaleas. The plant is well named, for it is as fragile as a baby's tear. A few steps will not kill it, but the footprint will remain for two or three days.

TAXUS

Yew
Coniferous shrub
Dense to light shade
Zones 5 to 8

While the species are large 40 to 50-foot trees, the many cultivars available are among the most useful coniferous evergreen shrubs for the landscape. Hardy and trouble-free, with handsome dark green foliage and a variety of dense, refined forms, almost their only drawback is overuse.

Like junipers, yews are often planted without consideration for their ultimate size. Your nursery will help you to select the appropriate variety, but be sure to ask how big it will grow. Yews accept formal pruning well and are often clipped into hedges or other shapes. Consider them also for massing, as an evergreen touch to the shrub border, and as a foundation plant. When allowed to develop their natural forms, the effect is usually graceful and appealing.

Give yews soil with excellent drainage and they will prove to be generally easy to grow and pest-free, in dense shade to filtered sun. In heavy, wet soils they will be stunted and sickly, if they survive at all. Give them adequate moisture and protect them from sweeping winds. In hot, dry climates, give them a northern exposure and hose the foliage frequently during the driest periods. Beware of their colorful, red fruits, the inner portions of which are poisonous.

Taxus baccata (English Yew; Hardy to Zone 7). This least hardy yew has several cultivars that are excellent for southern gardens.

Taxus cuspidata (Japanese Yew; Hardy to Zone 5). Many excellent cultivars of this species are available, ranging from a low, 1-foot-high and 3-foot-wide form with yellow new growth ('Aurescens') to a 40 to 50-foot pyramidal form ('Capitata').

Taxus × media (Anglojap Yew; Hardy to Zone 5). A hybrid between the above two species, this yew has an extremely wide variety of cultivars, from low, spreading types to tall, narrow ones.

THALICTRUM
ROCHEBRUNIANUM

Lavender Mist, Meadowrue
Perennial
Light shade
Hardy to Zone 5

These tall, airy plants have fine-textured foliage topped with delicate sprays of lavender flowers. Growing 3 to 6 feet high or more, this meadowrue makes a splendid background.

The flowers are lavender-violet with bright yellow stamens. Individually they are minute and have no petals; the showy parts are the purplish sepals and yellow stamens. They appear in great quantities in loose compound clusters, blooming in July and August.

The plant prefers deep, rich, moist soil that is high in organic matter. Light shade is best, but full sun is tolerated if the soil is kept moist. Space plants 24 inches apart. Meadowrue appreciates abundant water. It has few serious pests, but powdery mildew and rust are occasionally reported. It is best to divide the plant about every fifth year to relieve crowding of the root mass.

TORENIA FOURNIERI

Wishbone Flower
Annual
Dense to light shade

Quiet and unassuming, the wishbone flower is a little-known gem that should be a favorite of the discerning shade gardener. The individual flowers are especially interesting viewed up close: their structure is similar to that of the snapdragon, to which they are related, but the coloring is more reminiscent of the pansy. The upper petal is pale blue, the lower lip is deep violet, and the center is yellow. Newer varieties are tinged with pink or red. Two yellow stamens arch over the center in the shape of a wishbone, from which the plant receives its common name.

In the garden the plant forms a loose clump covered with tiny flowers. It is not a flashy flower by any means, and prefers a cool, damp retreat in a shady corner. Flowers fade quickly in bright sun and dry climate. Planted either in large beds as a ground cover, or dabbed here and there, the deep, cool colors with a slight yellow sparkle are particularly appropriate in dappled shade. Wishbone flowers prefer fertile, moist, fluffy soil that is high in organic matter, and dense to light shade. Keep them well watered. Before the first frost in the fall, dig them up, pot them, and bring them inside for winter color.

Tradescantia virginiana

Trillium grandiflorum

Trollius hybrids

TRADESCANTIA VIRGINIANA

Spiderwort
Perennial
Dense shade to full sun
Hardy to Zone 4

Adaptable to many difficult situations, including infertile soil, deep shade, and boggy conditions, the spiderwort will provide colorful blooms over a long season. However, it has a tendency to sprawl and ramble through the garden when it is not restrained. Named cultivars are usually superior to the native species.

The flowers are usually bright purple, although many varieties are white, blue, pink, or red. The blossoms are composed of three petals, are about 1 inch wide, and last individually for only a day; however, they are produced in clusters at the ends of the stems and bloom over a long season, from June to September.

The deep green leaves are straplike, growing to 1 inch wide and as long as 15 inches. The lower portion of the leaf is wrapped around the stem, giving the plant the appearance of a coarse grass. The form is variable but mostly upright; the plant is from 18 to 36 inches tall. The stems are angled at the joints. From midseason on, the plant will tend to sprawl into an open, tangled structure.

Spiderwort will spread enthusiastically by underground stems, and by aboveground stems that root where their joints contact the soil. It is long-lived, but requires frequent division to restrain its rampant growth.

Spiderwort tolerates nearly any soil, but grows most vigorously in moist, rich soils, which should be avoided by gardeners who desire to restrain the plant. Give it dense shade to full sun. Space plants 15 to 30 inches apart.

Spiderwort can be moderately difficult to restrain. It will look best with adequate water. If the stems flop badly in midsummer, they can be cut clear to the ground; the revived plant will flower again in the fall. It has few serious pests, although several types of caterpillars have been reported. Botrytis blight may attack the blossoms. Division is best performed every other year, and should be done at least every third or fourth year to restrain spreading. It is an excellent means of increase, and should be performed in the spring.

TRILLIUM

Wood Lily, Trillium
Perennial
Medium to light shade
Hardiness varies according to species

It is hard to imagine a woodland perennial more delightful than trillium. In earliest spring its smooth stems and furled foliage break through the leaf mold, and soon its handsome leaves, three to the stem, and three-petaled flower, centered among the leaves, provide one of the year's most special garden displays. Usually planted in informal clumps or groupings, it is at home among ferns and other woodland plants, around rocks in a shady nook, or nestled in a shaded border. Heights vary from 1 to nearly 3 feet. Trillium should, of course, be grown from seed (difficult sometimes) or purchased from a propagator, not dug from its dwindling numbers in the wild.

Flowers are solitary, and white, pink, or purplish. Like the leaves, the petals and sepals come in threes. The fruit is a large berry. The trio of leaves is clear green in some varieties and bronzy green or mottled in others. Foliage lasts through spring and summer.

Deep, rich, moist soil with high organic content is necessary. Drainage should be good. Medium shade in a cool spot is optimal, although most species grow well in somewhat deeper shade. Plant in autumn.

Care is easy, as long as trillium is properly situated and the soil is kept moist. Mulch annually. Snails and slugs like these juicy plants, so bait is often necessary. Tempting as trillium is for cutting, don't. Once the three leaves are gone, the plant has lost its means of sustenance.

Many species are available but not always easy to locate. The following are among the easiest to locate and grow.

T. chloropetalum (*T. sessile californicum*) (Giant Trillium; Hardy to Zone 7), native to Washington and California, is a big, showy plant. Its 12 to 30-inch stem bears big, dark green leaves mottled with bronze, and a flower whose 4-inch petals are erect and greenish, cream, rose, or mahogany.

T. erectum (Purple Trillium; Hardy to Zone 4), from eastern North America, actually bears deep red rather than purple flowers; some strains have white or yellowish flowers. Height is 10 to 12 inches. Each leaf is about 7 inches long. This is the most popular species for gardens.

T. grandiflorum (Trinity Flower, Wake Robin; Hardy to Zone 4) is another popular species, and one of the showiest. To 1½ feet high, it begins with shiny bronze growth and yellow buds, which develop into bright green foliage and a white flower, sometimes turning pinkish. Hard-to-find 'Flore Pleno' is many-petaled.

T. ovatum (Western Trillium; Hardy to Zone 8), native from British Columbia to California, grows to 1 or 1½ feet and has a large flower that opens white and turns rosy as it ages.

T. sessile (Toadshade; Hardy to Zone 6) is the eastern cousin of the western *T. chloropetalum*. Foliage is heavily mottled and veined. The maroon flower, growing directly out of the axis of the leaves, is erect, 2 inches long.

T. undulatum (Painted Trillium; Hardy to Zone 3), is named for its white flowers which are veined, mottled, or streaked with purple or rose. Petals are wavy. This foot-high species is from eastern North America.

TROLLIUS EUROPAEUS

Common Globe Flower
Perennial
Medium shade to full sun
Hardy to Zone 3

Globe flowers are leafy, bushy plants that produce rounded, globular blossoms in many shades of yellow and orange. Blooming in late spring and early summer, they are an excellent choice for

Tsuga canadensis 'Pendula'

Vancouveria chrysantha

the moist, heavy soils that most other perennials abhor.

Flowers come in many shades of yellow and orange, according to variety. They are 1 to 3 inches across and are composed of five to fifteen showy sepals in a rounded, ball-like mass that looks as if it has never fully opened. The flowers appear on the ends of long stems in May and June. The dark green leaves are deeply divided into three to five lobes. The basal leaves have stalks, and are larger and more dense than the stem leaves, whose bottom portions wrap around the stems. The stems grow 1 to 3 feet tall, depending upon variety, and in upright clusters, creating bushy, rounded masses. The foliage is attractive all season.

Globe flowers are long-lived and restrained in growth. The clumps gradually expand by sending up new shoots on the outside perimeter of the crown. Fertile, very moist soil that is high in organic matter is best, but avoid boggy conditions. While preferring medium or light shade, globe flowers will tolerate full sun if the soil is kept moist. Space plants 12 inches apart. Remove faded flowers to prolong the bloom period. Keep well watered, as these plants must never dry out. They have no serious pests. The plant usually requires division every five years or so to reduce crowding, but if necessary can survive much longer without disturbance. An excellent means of increase, division should be done in late summer.

TSUGA CANADENSIS 'PENDULA'

Sargent's Weeping Hemlock
Coniferous evergreen shrub
Light shade
Zones 4 to 8

This is the most commonly grown dwarf hemlock. It displays a graceful, pendulous habit and refined, evergreen foliage. While it can reach 5 to 6 feet in height and two or three times that in spread in extreme old age, a more reasonable size to expect is 3 to 4 feet high by 8 to 9 feet wide. This plant makes an outstanding focal specimen in a border, by an entryway, in a raised bed, or in a container.

Plant it in well-drained, moist, acid soil. Unlike most conifers it tolerates shade well, and in fact prefers light shade. If drainage is good, the soil is moist, and there are no drying winds, it will tolerate full sun. Hemlock will not tolerate wind, drought, or waterlogged soils, and in areas where summer temperatures exceed 95° it is likely to develop leaf scorch. This is not a plant for heavily polluted areas. If the location is right, however, hemlock is usually a trouble-free and long-lived plant.

VACCINIUM OVATUM

California Huckleberry
Deciduous shrub
Medium to light shade
Hardy to Zone 7

This handsome shrub pleases the palate as well as the eye of the gardener who chooses it. In medium to light shade it bears tasty, tart berries especially valued for pies, jams, and sauces. In heavy shade it produces little if any fruit, but its dark, evergreen foliage and some spring flowers more than justify its use in the garden. As an unpruned shrub it slowly grows to 5 to 10 feet. It can be pruned into hedges, and florists use its branches in wreaths and arrangements.

Flowers are ¼ inch long, bell-shaped, white or pinkish, in loose clusters toward the ends of twigs. They are replaced by ¼-inch berries that turn blackish as they ripen throughout autumn. The pinkish-bronze new growth matures into waxy, deep green leaves to 1¼ inches long. Foliage is dense and fine-textured, in flattish outward-leaning sprays. It contrasts pleasingly with the foliage of camellias and woodland plants like ferns, rhododendrons, and dogwood.

Huckleberry is native to the coastal redwood forests, wooded canyons, and stream areas of the West Coast, so it prefers shade and deep, acid soil with ample humus. Good drainage is desirable. A woodland-garden setting is ideal but not necessary, as long as basic cultural conditions are met. If the soil is not very acidic, add small amounts of aluminum sulfate and peat or other organic conditioner. Huckleberry is happiest with moisture but becomes drought-tolerant as it establishes. It is susceptible to scale.

V. angustifolium laevifolium (Blueberry; Hardy to Zone 2) is a deciduous fruit-bearing shrub of which many varieties are available. It requires light shade and moist, well-drained acid soil.

V. vitus-idaea (Cowberry; Hardy to Zone 2) is a creeping evergreen, to a foot high, suitable for small-area ground cover. *V. vitus-idaea minus* (Mountain Cranberry, Lingonberry), native to the northern United States and Canada, is a dwarf that forms dense mats 8 inches or lower and spreads by underground runners. The red berries of both forms make good preserves. Both are useful in wet, shaded areas.

VANCOUVERIA

American Barrenwort
Ground cover
Medium to light shade
Hardy to Zone 6

This Pacific Northwest native is closely related to the epimediums. American barrenwort (*V. hexandra*) grows to 1 or 1½ feet tall. White ½-inch flowers appear in May through June. The leaves are light green, delicate, and die to the ground each winter.

Vancouveria grows naturally in the shade of the coast redwoods, where the soil is acidic and high in organic matter. Temperatures are cool and there is plenty of moisture.

This is an excellent ground cover plant where it is well adapted. Combine with ferns and epimediums around the base of trees and in shaded beds. The cut foliage is attractive in bouquets.

Vinca major

Viola × wittrockiana

VINCA MINOR

Dwarf Periwinkle, Running Myrtle
Ground cover
Medium to light shade
Hardy to Zone 4

There is no more useful and versatile ground cover for the shade garden than dwarf periwinkle. This 6-inch-tall evergreen thrives in medium to light shade and produces healthy foliage, if few flowers, in deeper shade. It provides a cover for larger bulbs such as daffodil and tulip, and it is tall enough to hide withering bulb foliage. Its fast-growing runners can fill medium to large beds in a season. For covering shady slopes and trailing gracefully over walls and the edges of raised beds and planters, it is without equal.

Lavender-blue (periwinkle blue) flowers, an inch wide, appear toward the stem ends throughout the spring, and often longer. Their five fused petals seem to float starlike over the dark foliage. Oblong, glossy, deep green leaves are spaced at 1-inch intervals along the trailing stems. They remain evenly green throughout the year.

Plant periwinkles in shade and rich, moist, well-drained soil. As dwarf periwinkle is moderately aggressive, it is best used away from small, delicate plants. Set divisions or rooted cuttings 12 to 18 inches apart, preferably in the spring. Desert climates are too hot for it to flourish, even in the shade.

During the warm months, some moisture and about three feedings with a lawn fertilizer keep the foliage rich green and thick. Trim runners that grow out of bounds. To keep edges informal, prune stems individually. Occasional foot traffic does no harm.

V. m. 'Alba' has white flowers, *V. m.* 'Atropurpurea' has purple flowers. *V. m.* 'Aureomarginata' has blue flowers and leaves with bright, irregular, yellowish margins. The flowers of 'Bowles Variety' are deeper blue and larger than those of the species, and it is a more prolific bloomer. Its growth is slower because it spreads from expansion of the crown rather than rooting of trailing stems. 'Miss Jeckyll's White' is small-leafed, dainty, and very dwarf.

V. major is a larger, more upright and vigorous version of *V. minor*, 12 to 24 inches tall. It accepts more sun, more dryness, and less cold. Because it is so invasive, it should be used judiciously.

VIOLA ODORATA

Sweet Violet
Perennial
Medium to light shade
Hardy to Zone 6

Literary references to this most famous of the violas may be found from Homer to the literature of our age. Although not cultivated as widely as the pansy *(V. wittrockiana)*, it is probably most flower lovers' favorite viola—or violet, as most species except pansy are usually called. Scent alone would be reason enough for the popularity of this violet and its varieties. A broadly-clumping perennial that spreads by runners,

it is often used in light shade as a woodland ground cover or container plant. In all but the coldest winter climates it is evergreen. Heaviest flowering is in spring, but flowers may appear in other seasons.

The five-petaled flowers vary from deep purple to rose and white, depending on the variety. Most are single, but some are variegated and some are double. Most varieties have flowers ¾ inch across or larger. The leaves are heart-shaped, borne on the stems 2 to 8 inches long, depending on the variety.

Sweet violet likes cool, moist soil, reasonable drainage, and shade—ideally, light shade in cool climates, medium shade in hotter climates, even dense shade (with brightness) in desert areas. Air circulation aids in blooming. Acid, neutral, and slightly alkaline soils are good, as long as they are rich and friable. Pockets of sweet violet can grow beneath shallow-rooted trees.

Keep the soil moist, especially in lightly shaded or hot, dry spots. A winter covering of fallen leaves is good. Spider mites occasionally require spraying.

'Red Giant' has long-stemmed leaves, flower stems up to 10 inches, and red-violet flowers. 'Rosina' is 5 to 6 inches high. Its rosy pink flowers are profuse and especially fragrant; the leaves are downy. 'Royal Robe' grows up to 8 inches high, with large glossy leaves and deep violet-blue or purple flowers.

Different species of identical culture include the following:

V. alba (Parma Violet; Hardy to Zone 6) is popular for its intensely fragrant double flowers. It rapidly forms carpets of inch-wide leaves. Varieties are 'Lady

Hume Campbell' (lavender flowers marked with white) and 'Swanley White' (pure white flowers).

V. cornuta (Horned Violet, Tufted Violet, Viola; Hardy to Zone 6), from the Pyrenees, is a bedding plant quite close to the pansy in appearance, but smaller-flowered. Numerous hybrid forms are available. It can be grown from seed or set out as seedlings, 8 inches apart. Unlike most violas, it is treated as an annual. Light shade is best.

V. hederacea (Australian Violet; Hardy to Zone 7), a diminutive shade ground cover, is often available in nursery flats. It spreads rapidly by rooting runners. Leaves are tiny. Blue-and-white flowers are less than ½ inch wide, borne on 1 to 4-inch stems. It requires rich soil, moisture, and light shade. It is dormant in winter.

V. pedata (Bird's Foot Violet; Hardy to Zone 5), bearing 1½ inch violet to lilac-purple flowers with darker upper petals, is a striking spring bloomer. It thrives in well-drained but poor soil, in light shade. A rock garden setting is appropriate. In horticultural literature it is commonly termed the most beautiful of North American violets. Its name refers to the shape of its leaves.

V. priceana (Confederate Violet; Hardy to Zone 5) bears large, substantial, blue-veined white blossoms on long stems. Its heart-shaped leaves are 4 to 5 inches wide. It reseeds freely and makes a suitable ground cover for shrubs and larger woodland plants in medium shade. 'White Czar' has delicately-penciled purplish markings against a yellow blush at the center of large white flowers.

Index

Note: Italicized page numbers refer to illustrations.